Improving Composition

through a **Sentence Study** of **Grammar and Usage**

by Carol Compton

Educators Publishing Service, Inc.

Cambridge and Toronto

Educators Publishing Service, Inc.
75 Moulton Street, Cambridge, Massachusetts 02238-9101

REVISED EDITION, 1983
FIFTH PRINTING

Copyright © 1977, 1983 by Educators Publishing Service, Inc. All rights reserved. No part of this book may be reproduced or utilized in any form or by any electronic or mechanical means, including photocopying, without permission in writing from the publisher.
ISBN 0-8388-1596-0. Printed in U.S.A.

CONTENTS

INTRODUCTION

"In the final analysis,

a writer is as good as

his [or her] sentences."

—Percy Marks, *Better Themes*[1]

Purpose

This system is designed to help students improve their written expression through a comprehensive study of the sentence.

—It demonstrates that the sentence is the link between composition and grammar.

—It focuses on the significant aspects of grammar and usage as they relate in the sentence, the basic unit of composition.

—It demonstrates that the understanding of certain sentence elements, the grammatical functions and forms, and the proper use of these elements ensures effective written composition.

Simplified Approach

This system provides a simplified, sequential, three-part approach to understanding, to using, and to improving sentences.

—*Part I—Sentence Awareness:* emphasizes the need for sentence consciousness and the various ways "to see" a sentence.

—*Part II—Sentence Analysis:* provides a practical method to identify and to use the grammatical functions and forms and teaches grammar through writing as students "learn by doing."

—*Part III—Sentence Usage:* demonstrates a useful approach to understanding and to eliminating the "common errors" in English.
  —It shows that most errors occur because of the misapplication of grammatical principles.
  —It teaches the proper application of these grammatical principles for clear expression.
  —It helps students to become their own proofreaders.

Use

This system can be used in the following ways:
—as a separate course of study

—as an integral part of an existing course

—as an individualized study unit

—as a sequential departmental program extending across a number of grade levels.

Advantage

This system has one distinct advantage: it works.

Its basic concepts have been classroom tested successfully for many years. Students who have used this method successfully have attained higher scores on English achievement and proficiency tests; they have also communicated more effectively at college and at work.

TEACHING SUGGESTIONS

For additional suggestions see the *Teacher's Guide and Answer Key*.

This system is based on a three-part approach to sentence study.

Part I.   Sentence Awareness
Part II.   Sentence Analysis
Part III.   Sentence Usage

The approach is sequential and cumulative.

Explanations of sentence usage in Part III, for example, are based on specific terms introduced in Part I and stressed in Part II.

It is vital that students work through the materials in Part I and Part II before approaching the "Common Errors" in Part III.

Experience has shown that students who think that they have mastered the fundamentals (particularly the sentence functions) often have difficulties applying these fundamentals to the major forms in Part II and the common errors in Part III.

A thorough review is recommended, therefore, even for advanced or more mature students.

The sections that follow present specific teaching suggestions for each of the three parts.

PART I. SENTENCE AWARENESS

Significance

Part I is introductory and vital: it provides students with opportunities to acquire a practical perspective of the sentence and the necessary terminology for sentence study.

Approach

For beginning or less mature students, the best approach is to have the class read and discuss the questions and answers. For advanced or more mature students, alternatives range from participation in class discussions and independent study to participation in small-group and partner-discussions.

The grammatical terms in Section C present the greatest challenge, particularly to beginning students. (All students might benefit by keeping notebooks of grammatical terms in Parts I, II, and III.)

Section C provides students with a broad perspective, not an intensive study. The grammatical terms, therefore, should be introduced, not unduly stressed or belabored. Since an intense study of the significant functions and forms follows in Part II, the parts of speech, the clause, and the phrase should be looked at generally, not approached specifically at this time.

PART II. SENTENCE ANALYSIS

Significance

Part II focuses on the significant sentence functions and forms, the fundamentals necessary for understanding sentence relationships and using them with awareness. It stresses rules, rather than exceptions, and the necessary basics for working with sentence usage in Part III.

Approach

This section encourages students to identify and to use the necessary fundamentals. In conjunction with the vital *Test Questions*, the following should be stressed:

    Memorizing

        Students should know at least the following from memory:

the verb	action or linking (=)
	and the appropriate complements
the noun	the six specific functions in the proper order
the adjective	the adjective questions in the proper order
the adverb	the adverb questions in the proper order

    Identifying

        Students should be able to identify with ease the major forms:

the dependent clause	and its functions
the verbal phrase	and its functions

        The explanations of sentence usage in Part III greatly depend upon the understanding of these structures and their functions in sentences.

    Composing

        Students should write the composing exercises, for these exercises test their ability to use grammatical elements in sentences.

PART III. SENTENCE USAGE

Significance

Part III focuses on the "proper" and the "improper" relationships of the sentence functions and forms. It thus shows students how to apply grammatical principles to understand English usage. Since this section generally stresses the rule rather than the exception, specific instruction should deal with questions of "changing language usage" as they arise in particular classrooms.

Approach

The format of this section is sequential and cumulative. Students should master (A) (parallelism) before proceeding to (B) (case). The exercises following each chapter presuppose the mastery of the previous concepts. A three-part approach that has proved successful is as follows:

    I. A-H
        —the teaching individually of each concept A-H (with cumulative exercises interspersed)
        —the mid-point testing of concepts A-D
        —the major reviewing and testing of concepts A-H

    II. I-P
        —the teaching individually of each concept I-P (with cumulative exercises interspersed)
        —the mid-point testing of concepts I-L
        —the major reviewing and testing of concepts I-P

    III. A-P
        —the intensive reviewing of concepts A-P
        —the final testing of concepts A-P

PART I — SENTENCE AWARENESS

To gain deeper awareness of the sentence, students

must "see" the sentence from various points of view.

Part I emphasizes three ways "to see" the sentence: as an

independent structure, as a composite of main parts, and

as a composite of related functions and forms.

A. AWARENESS OF THE SENTENCE AS AN INDEPENDENT STRUCTURE

What is a sentence?

There are many definitions of the sentence. The following are representative examples:

> *A sentence is a complete thought.*
> —Traditional definition

> *A sentence is the expression of a single idea.*
> —Percy Marks, *Better Themes*[1]

> *The sentence is a single cry.*
> —Herbert Read, *English Prose Style*[2]

> *. . . the further back we went in the history of known languages, the more the sentence was one indissoluble whole . . .*
> —Otto Jespersen, *Language*[3]

Why are these definitions significant?

Like most definitions of the sentence, they stress a sense of wholeness or completeness.

Why is this sense of wholeness important?

Modern language experts like Jean Piaget have demonstrated that language learning proceeds from the whole to the part.[4] Knowing a sentence, for example, often precedes knowing many words.

> *Recent research suggests that before a child has learned many words, he has gained some knowledge of the basic structure of his language: the sentence. For instance, he may ask a question before he has acquired any intelligible words.*
> —Who's Afraid of Linguistics[5]

Why are these research findings significant for sentence study?

These research findings show the following:

—Sentence study concerns something that most students already know, for they have been thinking and using sentences since they were very young.

Most students must simply gain deeper awareness of that which they already know and constantly use.

2

—The natural way to study the sentence is the whole-to-part sequence.

Students must first "see" the sentence as an independent or a complete structure, the basic unit of composition, before they analyze the sentence to find its parts.

WORKING WITH THE SENTENCE AS AN INDEPENDENT STRUCTURE

CLASS ACTIVITIES

Recognizing

The following are sentences. They all express complete thoughts. Read them to "hear" their *completeness*.

He is a doctor.

Open the door.

The student played hockey.

Are you going to the game?

The package was opened by the teacher.

Composing

Write five sentences on different topics. Now test their completeness by reading them to another student who will "hear" whether or not they are complete. (Or read one sentence to the entire class to test its completeness.)

1.

2.

3.

4.

5.

Write five sentences using each of the following words in a sentence: *book, clock, car, drive, swing*.

1.

2.

3.

4.

5.

OTHER ACTIVITIES

Recognizing

1. Listen to others, and realize that they are speaking sentences. Write down the most important sentence that you have heard.

2. Bring to class the most entertaining sentence that you have heard in a media broadcast within the last twenty-four hours.

3. Bring to class the most interesting sentence that you have read in a written advertisement.

4. Bring to class the most dynamic sentence that you have read in a novel or in a text book.

5. Bring to class the most significant sentence that you have read in a newspaper or in a popular news magazine.

6. Reread your last composition. Bring to class the most thought-provoking sentence in that composition.

Composing

1. Keep a daily journal. Record in a single sentence your most meaningful experience or feeling.

2. Make a quotation booklet. Record ten significant sentences stated by famous people.

3. Make a sentence poster or collage focusing on an abstract concept such as *truth, beauty, loyalty, friendship*. Include both pictures and famous sentence quotations about the concept.

4. Write a dialogue in which two characters discuss a school problem; use complete sentences.

5. Record in a single sentence the most significant fact, idea, or concept that you have learned each day.

B. AWARENESS OF THE SENTENCE AS A COMPOSITE OF MAIN PARTS

Why does a sentence make sense?

It has been discovered that every sentence has two main parts:

—something (or someone) talked about
   Traditionally, it is called the *subject*.

—an action or state of being
   Traditionally, it is called the *verb*.
These two main parts, the subject and the verb, interact to form a complete thought.

How are these sentence parts usually found?

The verb, a word or word group that shows action or being, is usually the first element that is located.

The subject, the part talked about, usually answers the questions "who? or what?" before the verb.

s   v
The boy throws the ball.

Verb: *throws* — shows action
Subject: *boy* — answers the question "*Who* throws?"

s   v
A hobby is enjoyable.

Verb: *is* — shows being
Subject: *hobby* — answers the question "*What* is?"

What is the commonly used definition of a sentence?

A sentence is a group of words *containing a verb and its subject* and expressing a complete thought.

Is a single word ever a sentence?

Yes, a single *verb* sometimes represents a sentence. Its subject is not expressed; it is understood.

v
Stop.

Verb: *Stop.* — shows action
Subject: *You* — understood — answers the question "*Who* stops?"

Is any group of words that contains a verb and its subject a sentence?

No, some groups of words that contain a verb and its subject do not express complete thoughts.

        s   v
That she ran.   incomplete thought

          s   v
When you are ready.   incomplete thought

Remember that in conversation incomplete thoughts seem to make sense alone only because a sentence may be *partially expressed* but *wholly understood*.

Question: "When are we going to the game?"
Answer: "When you are ready." — The answer is a partially expressed thought but a wholly understood thought.
— The word group *When you are ready* really expresses the complete thought: "We are going to the game when you are ready."

What is one way to test for sentence completeness?

— Ask whether the group of words makes sense alone. Pretend, for example, that a person enters the classroom and makes a statement: "If we are to succeed." The statement is obviously incomplete.

— Use this questioning method on any group of words to test for sentence completeness.

WORKING WITH THE SENTENCE AS A COMPOSITE OF MAIN PARTS

Recognizing

1. The following are sentences. Write (v) over the verb; write (s) over the subject.

    Example: She is an attorney.

    (*s* over "She", *v* over "is")

    Students study in the cafeteria daily.

    The team won the last five games.

    Open the door quickly.

    He seems tired.

    She is a talented actress.

2. Some of the following are sentences; some are not. Write S before the word groups that are sentences.

    —That he will attend the dance.

    —Stop!

    —When you finish the project.

    —I am willing to participate in the athletic program.

    —Have you completed your French assignment yet?

Composing

1. Write a sentence in which you use the word *athlete* as subject and the word *ran* as verb.

2. Write a one word sentence.

C. AWARENESS OF THE SENTENCE AS A COMPOSITE OF RELATED FUNCTIONS AND FORMS

How are all of the related parts of a sentence usually identified?

They are identified through the study of grammar.

What is grammar?

There are many definitions of grammar. The definition that follows is useful because it emphasizes the significant relationship of sentence function and form.

> *GRAMMAR is the analysis of language*
> > *to indicate*
> *the functions of words in sentences*
> > *and*
> *the forms of words that show these functions.*
> > — *Proper Words in Proper Places*[6]

What is a sentence function?

A sentence function is the *use* of a word or word group in a particular sentence.

How are the sentence functions traditionally labeled?

They are labeled the *parts of speech.* A word or word group is labeled a *part of speech* according to its use or function in a particular sentence.

What are the eight parts of speech or sentence functions?

They are as follows:
1. the verb
2. the noun
3. the pronoun
4. the adjective
5. the adverb
6. the preposition
7. the conjunction
8. the interjection

Note: The Chart of Parts of Speech in *Appendix A* reviews specifically the main sentence functions. Only a general awareness of these terms is necessary at this point, for this system will review specifically the important sentence functions.

What is a sentence form?

It is a *sentence structure.* It is a word or word group that functions as part of a sentence.

What are the main sentence forms?

They are as follows: 1. the *word*
  the primary sentence structure
2. the *phrase*
  a word group
3. the *clause*
  a word group

How do the phrase and the clause, both word groups, differ?

A *phrase* is a group of two or more related words that functions as a sentence part.

s   v

Example: Ted *is singing*.

Phrase: *is singing*, two words used in this example as the verb

Note: The various types of phrases will be explained in Parts II and III.

A *clause* is a group of two or more related words *that contains a verb and its subject* and that functions as a sentence part.

There are two main types of clauses: the *independent clause** which expresses a complete thought and the *dependent clause* which expresses an incomplete thought.

Example: independent clause (i.c.)

s   v   s   v

Mary studies English and *her brother reads French*.
(i.c.)   (i.c.)

Each italicized word group is an independent clause.
Test: Each italicized sentence part* could be removed from the above sentence and stated as a separate sentence.

s   v

Mary studies English.   Complete Thought

s   v

Her brother reads French.   Complete Thought

Note: A sentence containing two or more independent clauses is called a compound sentence.

---

* Because the independent clause contains a verb with its subject and expresses a complete thought, some experts use the term *independent clause* interchangeably with the term *sentence*. Others use the term *independent clause* only when the word group is *part* of a sentence which contains at least one other clause, either dependent or independent. This system labels the independent clause a sentence part.

Example: dependent clause (d.c.)

$$\overset{s}{When} \overset{\quad v}{she \; entered} \; the \; room, \; \overset{s}{she} \; \overset{v}{saw} \; the \; statue.$$

The italicized word group is a dependent clause.

Test: The italicized sentence part could not be removed from the above sentence and stated as a separate sentence.

$$\overset{s}{When} \; \overset{v}{she \; entered} \; the \; room. \; Incomplete \; Thought$$

Note: A sentence containing one or more dependent clauses is called a complex sentence.

The clause will be explained further in Part II and Part III.

SIMPLIFIED APPROACH

Why are the terms function and form significant?

The terms *function* and *form* show a practical way of "talking about" words in sentences; they demonstrate, therefore, a simplified approach to the study of grammar.

There are only eight basic sentence functions: the parts of speech.

There are only three basic sentence forms: the word, the phrase, and the clause.

Awareness of the **relationship** of the eight **functions** and the three **forms** is the key to a grammatical understanding of the sentence.
—A sentence **form**, whether word, phrase, or dependent clause, always **functions** as a **part of speech**.

See the following Chart of Function and Form for an overview of the grammatical elements within a sentence.

CHART OF FUNCTION AND FORM

The terms *function* and *form* provide a dual way of looking at words (and word groups) in sentences.

The Sentence

Function	**Form**
(Use)	(Structure)

Function refers to the use of a word (or word group) in a particular sentence. A word (or word group) is labeled a part of speech according to its sentence function.

Form refers to the structure of a word (or word group) in a particular sentence. A sentence form represents an element that *functions* as part of a sentence, usually as a part of speech.

Eight Sentence Functions
(Parts of Speech)

1. Verb —————— Shows action or being.

2. Noun ————➤ Name
3. Pronoun

4. Adjective ————➤ Modify
5. Adverb

6. Preposition ————➤ Join
7. Conjunction

8. Interjection ——— Exclaims

Three Sentence Forms

1. Word
   The primary sentence structure used as a part of speech.

2. Phrase
   A word group — not containing a verb and its subject — used as a part of speech.

3. Clause
   A word group — containing a verb and its subject — used as part of a sentence. (A dependent clause always functions as a part of speech.)

How will this system further simplify the study of grammar?

PART II — SENTENCE ANALYSIS will emphasize a concentrated study of the major functions and forms, those functions and forms that constantly repeat and interrelate in sentences.

What are the major functions?

They are as follows: 1. the verb
                         2. the noun
                         3. the adjective
                         4. the adverb

What are the major forms?

They are as follows: 1. the dependent clause
                         2. the verbal phrase

How do these functions and forms relate?

A dependent clause or a verbal phrase always functions in a sentence as a noun, an adjective or an adverb. A verb, of course, is vital to any sentence.

WORKING WITH THE SENTENCE AS A
COMPOSITE OF RELATED FUNCTIONS AND FORMS

Remembering

Fill in the blanks with the appropriate words.

1. "Grammar is the analysis of language to indicate the _____ of words in _____ and the forms of words that show these functions."

2. Function refers to the _____ of a word in a particular sentence.

3. There are _____ (how many) sentence functions which are labeled the _____ of _____.

4. Form refers to the _____ of a word or word group in a particular sentence.

5. The three sentence forms are the _____, the _____, and the _____.

6. Awareness of the _____ of the sentence functions and forms is the key to a grammatical understanding of the sentence.

7. The study of grammar can be even further simplified by a concentrated study of the major _____ and _____.

8. The major functions are as follows: _____, _____, _____, _____.

9. The major forms are the dependent _____ and the verbal _____.

10. The major functions and forms relate in the sentence, since any major form always functions in a sentence as a (an) _____ , a (an) _____ , or a (an) _____ .

PART II — SENTENCE ANALYSIS

To become proficient at sentence analysis, students must know *what sentence elements to identify and what methods to use for their identification.* Part II emphasizes the significant sentence elements, the major functions and forms, and questioning techniques for their identification. It also provides opportunities for use of these elements in written composition.

A. MAJOR SENTENCE FUNCTIONS

Verbs, nouns, adjectives and adverbs . . . make up more

than ninety-nine percent of all words listed

in the dictionary.

—*Harbrace College Handbook*[1]

THE VERB

The verb is the heart of the sentence; without a verb no group of words is grammatically a sentence.
—*Harbrace College Handbook*[2]

What is a verb?

A verb is a word that shows action or linking in relation to its subject.

ACTION   The verb shows what the subject does.

$$
\begin{array}{cc} \text{s} & \text{v} \end{array}
$$

The coyote *howls*.

$$
\begin{array}{cc} \text{s} & \text{v} \end{array}
$$

The sea gull *eats* the clam.

The verb shows what happens to the subject.

$$
\begin{array}{cc} \text{s} & \text{v} \end{array}
$$

The clam *is eaten* by the sea gull.

LINKING   The verb links the subject with words following the verb.

$$
\begin{array}{cc} \text{s} & \text{v} \end{array}
$$

She *is* a doctor.

```
          s      v
He *appears* energetic.
```

Note: A linking verb is technically a type of state-of-being verb. Since the linking function is the common function of the state-of-being verb, this system will label state-of-being verbs as linking verbs.

A state-of-being verb can also simply show the subject existing.

```
s   v
I *am*. (I exist.)
```

How can a verb be identified in a particular sentence?

It can be identified with the **Test Questions for Verbs**.

TEST QUESTIONS FOR VERBS

■ **Does the sentence element show action or linking?**

ACTION   Does the sentence element show what the subject does?

```
            s      v
The child plays
     Verb: *plays* —shows action
```

LINKING   Does the sentence element merely link or connect the subject with other words in the sentence?

```
          s  v
The girl is a student.
     Verb: *is* — links *girl* with *student*
```

Common Linking Verbs

All forms of the verb *to be*: is, am, are, was, were, be, being, been
Other verbs: become, seem, appear, taste, feel, sound, grow

Note: Do not confuse *linking* verbs with *helping* verbs.

```
          s  v
1. He *is* a carpenter.
     Verb *is* — linking verb that connects *He* with *carpenter*.
```

           s v

2. He *is walking*.

    Verb *is* — helping verb that combines with a part of the action verb *walk* to form the verb phrase *is walking*, the verb of the sentence.

    Note: A verb phrase consists of two or more words used as a verb. (See the *Appendix* for additional information.)

INSTANT CHECK: Linking or Action

A linking verb is like an equal sign (=).

Whatever follows a linking verb either renames (equals) the subject or describes (modifies) the subject.

    s   v

Tim is a teacher. Tim equals a teacher. *Teacher* renames Tim.
    (=)

    s   v

Tim is handsome. Tim equals handsome. *Handsome* describes Tim.
    (=)

An action verb is not an equal sign (≠).

Tim washes the car. Tim does not equal (≠) the car.

Note: Some verbs can function as either action or linking verbs depending upon their use in a particular sentence.

      s   v

The girl tastes the apple.
    Verb: *tastes* — shows action
        The girl ≠ the apple.

      s   v

The apple tastes good.
    Verb: *tastes* — links
        The apple = good.

■ **If the verb shows action, does the verb have complements: words that usually follow the verb and help to complete its action?**

Some action verbs have complements; some need no complements.

Complement: Direct Object

—A noun called the direct object (do) completes the action of the verb.
The direct object answers the question "*whom* or *what?*" after the verb.

```
  s      v      do
Tom helps Maria.
```

Verb:	*helps* — shows action
Direct Object:	*Maria* — answers the question "helps *whom?*"

```
  s      v      do
Tom drives his car.
```

Verb:	*drives* — shows action
Direct Object:	*car* — answers the question "drives *what?*"

Complement: Indirect Object

—A noun called the indirect object (io) may also be present. An indirect object answers the question "*to* or *for whom* or *what?*"

```
   s        v      io      do
Rhonda bought Susan the book.
```

Verb:	*bought* — shows action
Direct Object:	*book* — answers the question "bought *what?*"
Indirect Object:	*Susan* — answers the question "for *whom?*"

```
  s     v     io          do
Rico gave the car a second coat of polish.
```

Verb:	*gave* — shows action
Direct Object:	*coat* — answers the question "gave *what?*"
Indirect Object:	*car* — answers the question "to *what?*"

Note: An indirect object can be present only if there is a direct object. Something must be received directly before it can be received indirectly.

ACTION VERB
WITHOUT
COMPLEMENTS

—The action verb needs no completer or complement.

       s   v
The bell rings.

       s   v
The horse runs swiftly.

Note: The word *swiftly* answers the question "*how?*" not the question "*what?*". It is not a sentence complement.

■ **If the verb shows linking, does the linking verb have a complement?**

Yes, all linking verbs have complements, since the "linking" function is to connect the subject with words in the verb part of the sentence.

Complement: Predicate Noun
—A noun which follows a linking verb is called a predicate noun (pn). It is a noun in the verb — predicate — part of the sentence which renames the subject.

      s   v   pn
Karen is an athlete.
       (=)

          Verb: *is* — links

          Predicate Noun: *athlete* — renames Karen

Complement: Predicate Adjective
—An adjective which follows a being or linking verb is called a predicate adjective (pa). It is an adjective in the verb — predicate — part of the sentence which refers to or describes the subject.

      s   v   pa
Mary appears intelligent.
        (=)

          Verb: *appears* — links

          Predicate Adjective: *intelligent* — describes Mary

                   intelligent Mary

```
┌─────────────────────────────────────────────────────────────────────────────┐
│                                                                               │
│            INSTANT CHECK: Predicate Noun or Predicate Adjective               │
│                                                                               │
│   A predicate noun is something (or someone) that can be talked about.        │
│                                                                               │
│              s    v        pn                                                 │
│           Mike is an electrician.        One can talk about an electrician.   │
│                (=)                                                            │
│                                                                               │
│   A predicate adjective cannot be talked about.                              │
│                                                                               │
│              s   v     pa                                                     │
│           Ann is beautiful.              One cannot talk about a beautiful.   │
│                (=)                                                            │
│                                                                               │
│                                                                               │
│   Remember:  Only a predicate noun or a predicate adjective can complete a    │
│   linking verb (=).                                                          │
│                                                                               │
└─────────────────────────────────────────────────────────────────────────────┘
```

Therefore, in summary, what are the four sentence complements?

The four sentence complements of verbs are as follows:

```
      the direct object ─────
            and                 ───> following an action verb
      the indirect object ─────

      the predicate noun ─────
            and                 ───> following a linking verb
      the predicate adjective ──
```

REVIEW

Test Questions for Verbs

■ **Does the verb show action or linking?**

	s v
ACTION:	Mary threw the ball.

	s v
LINKING:	Joshua is a pilot
	(=)

■ **If the verb shows action, does the verb have complements: a direct object and (possibly) an indirect object?**

ACTION VERB
WITH
COMPLEMENTS

        s   v   do
Jane wrote a letter.

        s   v   io   do
Carl gave Mike the cards.

ACTION VERB
WITHOUT
COMPLEMENTS

      s   v
She walked slowly

■ **If the verb shows linking, is the complement a predicate noun or a predicate adjective?**

LINKING VERB
WITH
PREDICATE NOUN

         s   v   pn
The stranger is a journalist.
         (=)

LINKING VERB
WITH
PREDICATE ADJECTIVE

         s   v   pa
The stranger seems happy.
         (=)

WORKING WITH VERBS

Remember to use the **Test Questions for Verbs**.

Recognizing

Directions:
1. Identify each verb and its subject in the sentences below by placing *v* over the verb and *s* over the subject.
2. Identify each linking verb by placing an equal sign (=) under it.
3. Identify any complement by placing the appropriate abbreviation over it: do, io, pn, pa.

$$\begin{array}{cccc} & s & v & pn \end{array}$$
Example: She is an investigator.
$$(=)$$

1. Rhonda is a librarian.

2. Tim gave Maureen the tickets.

3. Susan feels happy.

4. She dropped the vase.

5. The athlete ran swiftly.

6. Gail gave Dennis the message.

7. Ted seems angry.

8. The pitcher threw the ball.

9. Booker plays the piano.

10. She is a golfer.

Composing

Directions: Write one sentence to illustrate each numbered element below. Identify each verb, subject, and complement by placing the appropriate abbreviation over it.

Example: a linking verb completed by a predicate noun

```
      s   v    pn
She is a lawyer.
      (=)
```

1. an action verb without complements

2. an action verb completed by a direct object

3. a linking verb completed by a predicate noun

4. an action verb completed by a direct object and an indirect object

5. a linking verb completed by a predicate adjective

6. the word *taste* as a linking verb

7. the word *book* as a direct object

8. the word *desk* as a predicate noun

9. the word *taste* as an action verb

10. the word *plant* as an action verb

THE NOUN

What is a noun?

A noun is a word or word group that names a person, place, thing, quality, idea, or action.

How can a noun be identified in a particular sentence?

It can be identified with the **Test Questions for Nouns**.

TEST QUESTIONS FOR NOUNS

■ **Is the sentence element something (or someone) that can be "talked about"?**

The *truth* is evident.

> Noun: *truth* — names a quality
> One can talk about *truth*.

Skiing is invigorating.

> Noun: *skiing* — names an action
> One can talk about *skiing*.

That she is honest is obvious.

> Noun: *that she is honest* — names an idea
> One can talk about the idea *that she is honest*

Note: The pronoun *it* can be substituted for a noun.

> *That she is honest* is obvious.
> *It* is obvious.

■ Does the element serve one of the specific noun functions?

Note: The subject and the complements have already been reviewed.

1. Subject (s)

    s   v
    Tim is a sailor.
      (=)

2. Predicate noun (pn)

    s   v   pn
    Tim is a sailor.
      (=)

3. Appositive (app)
   (A noun that directly follows another noun and renames it.)

    s   app   v
    Ginger, my collie, can perform
    many tricks.

4. Direct object (do)

    s   v   do
    She swatted the fly.

5. Indirect object (io)

    s   v   io   do
    Mary gave Tim the sandwich.

6. Object of preposition (op)
   (A noun that answers the question "what or whom?" after a preposition.)

    s   v   p   op
    Mary won the award for accuracy.

WORKING WITH NOUNS

Remember to use the **Test Questions for Nouns**.

Memorizing

Directions: Memorize the six noun functions in the order listed:

1. s   4. do
2. pn   5. io
3. app   6. op

Recognizing

Directions: Identify the following in each sentence below:

1. The verb (v); the subject (s); each linking verb (=).
2. Any complements: do, io, pn, pa
3. Any remaining noun functions: app or op

<pre>
            s   v   op
Example: The children work in the garden.
</pre>

1. The teacher, a friend, is a talented person.

2. Barbara gave Helen the package.

3. The reason for study is obvious.

4. Jim gave Ron the message.

5. Mr. Alvarez, a lawyer, lives in the city.

6. Jim gave the message to Ron.

7. Angela spent the money on books.

8. The family traveled in Mexico.

9. Lill attended the concert at Lincoln Center.

10. The dog is a poodle.

Composing

Directions: Write one sentence to illustrate each numbered element listed below. Identify each verb and its subject and all other noun functions with the appropriate abbreviations.

Example: the word *girl* as the subject

s   v   do

The girl drank the lemonade.

1. the word *boy* as the subject

2. the word *student* as a predicate noun

3. the word *pilot* as an appositive

4. the word *gift* as a direct object

5. the word *girl* as an indirect object

6. the word *classroom* as an object of the preposition

7. a direct object

8. an appositive

9. a subject of a linking verb

10. a subject of an action verb

THE ADJECTIVE

What is an adjective?

An adjective is a modifier. It is a word or word group that modifies — describes or tells more about — a noun or a pronoun.

How can an adjective be identified in a sentence?

It can be identified with the **Test Questions for Adjectives.**

TEST QUESTIONS FOR ADJECTIVES

■ **Does the sentence element tell more about a noun or a pronoun?**

The *talented* musician played in the concert.

> Adjective: *talented* — tells more about the noun *musician*

She is *happy*.

> Adjective: *happy* — tells more about the pronoun *she*

■ **Does the sentence element answer one of the adjective questions: which, what kind of, how many, whose?**

Which?
> The *red* dress has been sold.
> > Adjective: *red* — answers the question "*which* dress?"

What Kind Of?
> The *small* boy seemed lost.
> > Adjective: *small* — answers the question "*what kind of* boy?"

How Many?
> *Five* scouts received awards.
> > Adjective: *five* — answers the question "*how many*" students?

Whose?
> *Her* house has been purchased.
> > Adjective: *her* — answers the question "*whose* house?"

Remember: *Which, what kind of, how many,* and *whose*
Are the adjective questions for you to choose.

31

WORKING WITH ADJECTIVES

Remember to use the **Test Questions for Adjectives.**

Memorizing

Directions: Memorize the adjective questions in the following order: *which? what kind of? how many? whose?*

Recognizing

Directions: Identify the following in each sentence below:
1. The verb, its subject, and any linking verb (=)
2. Any complements: do, io, pn, pa
3. Any adjectives: adj
   Draw an arrow from the adjective to the word modified and write the adjective question answered on the line at the right.

adj   s   v
Example: The black cat returned.   <u>which?</u>

1. Two detectives solved the mystery.   _____

2. He was a powerful monarch.   _____

3. Her sister is attending a lecture.   _____

4. The red car won the race.   _____

5. Her brother works enthusiastically.   _____

Composing

Directions: Write one sentence to illustrate each numbered element that follows. In each sentence, identify the verb, its subject, and any adjective. Draw an arrow from the adjective to the word modified.

Example: an adjective answering the question
which?

adj   s   v
The dynamic speaker was applauded.

1. an adjective answering the question *whose?*

2. an adjective modifying the subject

3. an adjective answering the question *how many?* and modifying the direct object

4. an adjective modifying the predicate noun

5. an adjective answering the question *which?* and modifying an appositive

6. the word *safe* as an adjective modifying a direct object

7. the word *five* as an adjective modifying the subject

8. the word *intelligent* as an adjective modifying the object of a preposition

9. the word *competent* as a predicate adjective

10. the word *true* as an adjective modifying a predicate noun

THE ADVERB

What is an adverb?

An adverb is a modifier. It is a word or word group that modifies — tells more about — a verb, another adverb, or an adjective.

How can an adverb be identified in a particular sentence?

It can be identified with the **Test Questions for Adverbs**

TEST QUESTIONS FOR ADVERBS

■ **Does the sentence element modify — tell more about — a verb, another adverb, or an adjective?**

Note: There are memory clues in the word *adverb.*
Ad*verb*: Modifies a verb
*Ad*verb: Modifies another adverb
Adverb: Modifies an adjective, the only other modifier

Carole ran *swiftly.*
Adverb: *swiftly* — modifies the verb *ran*

Carl plays the bass guitar *extremely* well.
Adverb: *extremely* — modifies the adverb *well.*

The salesperson is *very* tired.
Adverb: *very* — modifies the adjective *tired.*

■ **Does the sentence element answer one of the adverb questions: how, when, where, why, how much?**

How?

      s   v   adv
Carole ran *swiftly.*
     Adverb: *swiftly* — answers the question "ran *how?*"

When?

      s   v   adv
He left *immediately.*
     Adverb: *immediately* — answers the question "left *when?*"

Where?

 s   v   adv
He looked *everywhere* for his slippers.
 Adverb: *everywhere* — answers the question "looked *where?*"

Why?

adv v   s   v
Why are you leaving?
 Adverb: *Why* — deals with the question "are leaving *why?*"

How Much?

 s   v   adv   v
She has *almost* finished her homework.
 Adverb: *almost* — answers the question "*how much* or *to what degree* finished?"

Remember: *How, when, where, why* and *how much*
 Are the adverb questions to use as a crutch.

WORKING WITH ADVERBS

Remember to use the **Test Questions for Adverbs**

Memorizing

Directions: Memorize the adverb questions in the following order: *how? when? where? why? how much?*

Recognizing

Directions: Identify the following in each sentence below:
1. The verb, its subject, and any linking verb (=)
2. Any adjectives: adj
3. Any adverbs: adv
   Draw an arrow from the adverb to the word modified and write the adverb question answered on the line at the right.

                          s   v   adv
Example: He walked slowly.   <u>how?</u>

1. Peter ran swiftly.   _____

2. The messenger left immediately.   _____

3. Rebecca was very happy.   _____

4. Why did Sandra leave?   _____

5. The child looked everywhere.   _____

Composing

Directions: Write one sentence to illustrate each numbered element below. After identifying the verb and its subject in each sentence, identify any adjective or adverb and draw a line from it to the word modified.

Example: an adverb modifying a verb.

s   v   adv
He worked quickly.

1. an adverb answering the question *how?*

2. an adverb modifying the verb and answering the question *when?*

3. an adverb modifying a predicate adjective

4. an adverb modifying another adverb

5. an adverb answering the question *where?*

6. the word *slowly* as an adverb modifying the verb

7. the word *very* modifying a predicate adjective

8. the word *soon* as an adverb modifying the verb

9. the word *eagerly* as an adverb modifying the verb

10. the word *south* as an adverb modifying the verb

THE MODIFYING PHRASES

What then are the modifiers?

The modifiers are the adjective and the adverb.

What is a modifying phrase?

It is a phrase, a group of two or more words, that functions in a sentence as an adjective or an adverb. It should be placed as close as possible to the word(s) it modifies.

What is a common modifying phrase?

The prepositional phrase is one type of phrase that commonly functions as an adjective or an adverb. A prepositional phrase consists of a preposition, its object, and any modifiers of the object.

He walked *on thin ice*.

Prepositional Phrase:	on thin ice
Preposition:	on
Object:	ice — noun answers the question *"on what?"*
Modifier of Object:	thin — adjective telling *"what kind* of ice?"
Function of Phrase:	adverb — answers the question "walked (v) *where?*"

How then is the function of a prepositional phrase usually identified in a sentence?

It is usually identified with the **Test Questions for Adjective or Adverb Phrases**

TEST QUESTIONS FOR ADJECTIVE PHRASES

■ **Does the prepositional phrase modify a noun or pronoun? Does it answer an adjective question?**

The boy *with the clarinet* attended the music festival.

Prepositional Phrase:	with the clarinet
Function:	adjective — modifies the noun *boy*
	— answers the question *"which* boy?"

TEST QUESTIONS FOR ADVERB PHRASES

■ **Does the prepositional phrase modify a verb, an adverb, or an adjective? Does it answer an adverb question?**

She raced *in the park*.

Prepositional Phrase: in the park

Function: adverb — modifies the verb *raced*
                                   — answers the question "raced *where?*"

WORKING WITH MODIFYING PHRASES

Recognizing

Directions: Using the appropriate test questions, identify the following in the sentences below:
1. Each verb, its subject, and each linking verb (=).
2. Any sentence complements: do, io, pn, pa
3. Any phrase modifiers: adjective or adverb.
   Underline each prepositional phrase.
   Label it *adj* or *adv* and draw a line from it to the word it modifies.
   Write the adjective or adverb question on the line provided.

s   v   adv
Example: He works in the city.   where?

1. The girl in the front row is my sister.   _____

2. He lives in a small town.   _____

3. She will succeed because of her persistence.   _____

4. They returned at dawn.   _____

5. Boise is the capital of Idaho.   _____

Composing

Directions: Write one sentence to illustrate each numbered element that follows. Identify the type of phrase by underlining it and writing *adj* or *adv* above it. Draw an arrow to the word it modifies.

Example: an adjective phrase modifying the direct object

s   v   adj
She bought the dress on the center rack.

1. an adverb phrase modifying the verb *swam*

2. an adjective phrase modifying a predicate noun

3. an adverb phrase answering the question *where?*

4. an adjective phrase modifying the subject *student*

5. an adverb phrase answering the question *when?*

REVIEW OF MAJOR FUNCTIONS

What then are the major sentence functions?

They are the verb, the noun, the adjective, and the adverb.

What is the most important question to ask about a verb?

Does the verb show action or linking?

What are the possible complements of a verb?

They are as follows:
the direct object
and   following an action verb
the indirect object

the predicate noun
and   following a linking verb
the predicate adjective

What are the six main noun functions?

They are as follows:
1. subject
2. predicate noun
3. appositive
4. direct object
5. indirect object
6. object of preposition

Note: Observe again that all noun functions except the appositive and the object of the preposition relate directly to the verb.

What is an adjective?

It is a modifier of a noun or a pronoun.

What are the adjective questions in the proper order?

They are as follows: which? what kind of? how many? whose?

What is an adverb?

It is a modifier of a verb, an adjective, or an adverb.

What are the adverb questions in the proper order?

They are as follows: how? when? where? why? how much?

41

PROCEDURE FOR BASIC SENTENCE ANALYSIS

What then, in review, is the procedure for basic sentence analysis?

The procedure is to ask the right questions to identify the following:

1. The verb and its subject
2. The verb function: action or linking
3. Any complements: direct object, indirect object
    predicate noun, predicate adjective
4. Any modifiers: adjectives or adverbs

Note: *Analyzing* is "breaking down" to find the parts of a whole (sentence).
Composing is "building up" to create the parts of a whole (sentence).
When composing, use the analysis procedure in reverse.
— Select a verb (action or linking) and its subject.
— Choose appropriate complements and modifiers.
— Work with *awareness* of the sentence elements.

How does the "Procedure for Basic Sentence Analysis" prepare students for their forthcoming study of the major sentence forms?

— It demonstrates that *any* sentence has the same basic parts: the *verb* (action or linking); its *subject;* any *complements;* any *modifiers.*

— Whether a sentence contains words or word groups such as the major forms its basic parts remain the same.

What should students realize as they work with the major forms?

They should realize how frequently they themselves use these repeating word groups in their own spoken and written communications.

What then is the forthcoming challenge for most students?

Most students must simply learn to recognize and to use *consciously* those word groups that they now use *automatically.*
Their conscious use of these elements will give students better control of their own sentences.

B. MAJOR SENTENCE FORMS

The dependent clause and the verbal phrase

are word groups used commonly

in spoken and written expression.

THE DEPENDENT CLAUSE

What is a dependent clause?

A dependent clause is a word group that contains a verb and its subject and that expresses an incomplete thought.

It usually also contains a beginning word, an introductory word that frequently precedes the subject, and any related complements and modifiers.

It functions in a sentence as a noun, an adjective, or an adverb. A dependent clause is labeled, therefore, a *noun clause*, an *adjective clause*, or an *adverb clause*.

THE NOUN CLAUSE

What is a noun clause?

A noun clause is a dependent clause that functions in a sentence as a noun. Noun clauses often begin with words such as the following:

that, whose	whoever, whatever, whichever
who, what, which	when, where

How can a noun clause be identified in a particular sentence?

It can be identified with the **Test Questions for Noun Clauses.**

TEST QUESTIONS FOR NOUN CLAUSES

■ **Is the word group a dependent clause?** (Does it contain a beginning word, a verb, its subject, and any related complements and modifiers? Does it express an incomplete thought?)

      s   v

I know *that you will succeed*.

Word Group:	that you will succeed
Beginning Word:	that
Verb:	will succeed
Subject:	you — answers the question "*who* will succeed?"
Related Words:	none
Incomplete Thought:	Yes: the word group does not make sense alone.

      s   v

Maura believes *that ambitious students achieve excellence*.

Word Group:	that ambitious students achieve excellence
Beginning Word:	that
Verb:	achieve
Subject:	students
Modifier:	ambitious — adjective telling "*what kind* of students?"
Complement:	excellence — direct object answering the question "*achieve what?*"
Incomplete Thought:	Yes: the word group does not make sense alone.

Note: The beginning word is sometimes omitted.
      Maura believes *ambitious students achieve excellence*.
      (The beginning word *that* has been omitted.)

Note: The beginning word is sometimes the subject.
      Give *whoever calls* the message.

Word Group:	whoever calls
Beginning Word:	whoever — the subject of the clause
Verb:	calls
Subject:	whoever — the beginning word

44

INSTANT CHECK: Clause Completeness

Sometimes clause completeness can be checked effectively by eliminating what seems to be the clause and then reading the remaining words for sentence sense.

Maura believes *that ambitious students achieve* excellence.
The italicized word group might represent what a student thought the clause to be.
The remaining sentence would then read as follows:
Maura believes excellence. This word group lacks sense. The complement *excellence* obviously belongs in the clause.

■ **Does the word group function in the sentence as a noun?** (Does it serve one of the main noun functions?)

1. Subject (s)

         s   v
That she succeeded is true.

2. Predicate noun (pn)

         s   v   pn
The truth is that she succeeded.

3. Appositive (app)

       s   app   v
The truth that she succeeded is obvious.

4. Direct object (do)

    s   v   do
I know that she succeeded.

5. Indirect object (io)

        v   io
Give whoever calls the news.

6. Object of preposition (op)

      s   op   v
The reason for what he said is evident.

INSTANT CHECK: Noun Clause

Note: The pronoun *it* can usually be substituted for the clause.

    That he succeeded is true.
    It is true.

WORKING WITH NOUN CLAUSES

Remember to use the **Test Questions for Noun Clauses**

Recognizing

Directions: After identifying the verb and its subject, identify each noun clause in the sentences below by underlining the clause. Write the function of the clause above it.

<pre>
                        s   v
Example: That we will win is obvious.
</pre>

1. I know that you are happy.

2. Give whoever calls, the answer.

3. That she is enthusiastic is true.

4. The rumor that he left the company is false.

5. The reason for what she said is obvious.

6. The reason for his credibility was that he had spoken truthfully.

7. The teacher realizes that you have worked diligently.

8. That it is raining is obvious.

9. The gist of what we learned is evident.

10. We understand what you have written.

Composing

Directions: Write one sentence to illustrate each of the numbered elements below. After identifying each verb and its subject, underline each clause and write its function above it.

Example: a noun clause beginning with *that* as subject.

s   v
<u>That this exercise is easy</u> is true.

1. a noun clause as the subject

2. a noun clause as a direct object

3. the noun clause *that she is happy* as an appositive

4. the noun clause *that he is happy* as a predicate noun

5. a noun clause beginning with *whoever* as an indirect object

6. a noun clause beginning with *what* as the object of the preposition

7. a noun clause as a predicate noun

8. the noun clause *whoever calls* as an indirect object

9. the noun clause *whoever calls* as the subject

10. the noun clause *what the teacher said* as an object of a preposition

THE ADJECTIVE CLAUSE

What is an adjective clause?

An adjective clause is a dependent clause that functions in a sentence as an adjective. Adjective clauses frequently begin with words such as the following:

who, whom, whose
which, that
where, when

How can an adjective clause be identified in a particular sentence?

It can be identified with the **Test Questions for Adjective Clauses.**

TEST QUESTIONS FOR ADJECTIVE CLAUSES

■ **Is the word group a dependent clause?** (Does it contain a beginning word, a verb, its subject, and any related modifiers and complements? Does it express an incomplete thought?)

s   v
The house *that I like* is a colonial.

Word Group:	that I like
Beginning Word:	that
Verb:	like
Subject:	I
Related Words:	none
Incomplete Thought:	Yes: The word group does not make sense alone.

Note: The beginning word is sometimes omitted.
This is the book *I like best.*

(The word *that* has been omitted.)

Note: An adjective clause is sometimes called a *relative clause* because the beginning word is frequently a relative pronoun, a word that stands for a noun or pronoun in the main part of the sentence.

It is he *whom I trust.*

Relative Pronoun: *whom* — refers to the pronoun *he*, the antecedent of *whom*

Note: The beginning word is sometimes the subject.

s   v

The person *who drives recklessly* endangers others.

Word Group:	who drives recklessly
Beginning Word:	who — the subject of the clause
Verb:	drives
Subject:	who — the word that begins the clause
Modifiers:	recklessly — adverb answering the question "drives how?"
Incomplete Thought:	Yes: the word group does not make sense alone.

■ **Does the word group function in the sentence as an adjective?** (Does it modify a noun or a pronoun? Does it answer an adjective question?)

s   v

The boy *who reported to the office* is my cousin.

Word Group:	who reported to the office — dependent clause
Function:	adjective — modifies the noun *boy*
	— answers the question "*which* boy?"

WORKING WITH ADJECTIVE CLAUSES

Remember to use the **Test Questions for Adjective Clauses.**

Recognizing

Directions: After identifying each verb and its subject in the sentences below, underline each adjective clause and draw an arrow from the clause to the word modified.

Example: The student who studies will succeed.

1. Ms. Brown is the person who wrote the bestseller.

2. The novel that I like best is *The Red Badge of Courage.*

3. The senator who arrived late is her cousin.

4. The problem which has been identified will be solved.

5. The time when we should unite is now.

6. The house where she was born has been destroyed.

7. The archer whose aim is most accurate will hit the bullseye.

8. We saw the woman who bought the car.

9. The student whom we recognized registered today.

10. Activities that are useful will be added to the program.

Composing

Directions: Write one sentence to illustrate each numbered element listed below. In each sentence, underline the adjective clause and draw an arrow to the word it modifies. Remember to first identify each verb and its subject.

Example: *who lives in New York* as an adjective modifying the subject

The boy who lives in New York won the contest.

1. an adjective clause modifying a direct object

2. an adjective clause modifying the subject

3. an adjective clause answering the question *which?*

4. an adjective clause modifying a predicate noun

5. the adjective clause *who attends college* modifying the subject

6. an adjective clause beginning with *which*

7. an adjective clause beginning with *where*

8. the adjective clause *that I like* modifying the direct object

9. an adjective clause that begins with *whose*

THE ADVERB CLAUSE

What is an adverb clause?

An adverb clause is a dependent clause that functions in a sentence as an adverb. Adverb clauses frequently begin with words that answer the adverb questions:

ADVERB QUESTIONS	BEGINNING WORDS
How?	as, as if
When?	when, while, after
Where?	where
Why?	because, since, so that
How Much? (to what extent?)	than
On What Condition?	until, if

Note: A word that begins an adverb clause, thus joining the incomplete or subordinate clause to the main part of the sentence, is called a *subordinating conjunction.*

How can an adverb clause be identified in a particular sentence?

It can be identified with the **Test Questions for Adverb Clauses.**

TEST QUESTIONS FOR ADVERB CLAUSES

■ **Is the word group a dependent clause?** (Does it contain a beginning word, a verb, its subject, and any related modifiers and complements? Does it express an incomplete thought?)

When she had finished her homework, she watched television.

(with s over "she" and v over "had finished")

Word Group:	When she had finished her homework
Beginning Word:	When
Verb:	had finished
Subject	she
Complement:	homework — direct object answering the question "had finished *what?*"
Modifier:	her — adjective answering the question "*whose home-work?*"
Incomplete Thought:	Yes: the word group does not make sense alone.

52

INTRODUCTORY ADVERB CLAUSE

Note: An introductory adverb clause is one that precedes the subject and the verb of the sentence.
It is usually followed by a comma.

$$\overset{\text{s}}{\textit{If you}} \overset{\text{v}}{\textit{are ready}}, \text{ we shall leave.}$$

Introductory Clause:	$\overset{\text{s}}{\text{If you}} \overset{\text{v}}{\text{are}}$ ready
Comma:	Follows the dependent clause

■ **Does the word group function in the sentence as an adverb?** (Does it modify a verb, an adverb, or an adjective? Does it answer an adverb question?)

$$\overset{\text{s}}{\text{He}} \overset{\text{v}}{\text{walked}} \textit{ as if he were very tired.}$$

Word Group:	$\text{as if } \overset{\text{s}}{\text{he}} \overset{\text{v}}{\text{were}} \text{ very tired}$ — dependent clause
Function:	adverb — modifies the verb *walked* — answers the question "walked *how?*"

$$\overset{\text{s}}{\text{He}} \overset{\text{v}}{\text{watched}} \text{ television } \textit{when he had finished his assignments.}$$

Word Group:	$\text{when } \overset{\text{s}}{\text{he}} \overset{\text{v}}{\text{had}} \text{ finished his assignments}$ — dependent clause
Function:	adverb — modifies the verb *watched* — answers the question "watched *when?*"

$$\overset{\text{s}}{\text{They}} \overset{\text{v}}{\text{settled}} \textit{ where they could build a home.}$$

Word Group:	$\text{where } \overset{\text{s}}{\text{they}} \overset{\text{v}}{\text{could}} \text{ build a home}$ — dependent clause
Function:	adverb — modifies the verb *settled* — answers the question "settled *where?*"

   s   v

She worked *so that she could buy a car*.

                                      s   v

Word Group: so that she could buy a car

Function: adverb — modifies the verb *worked*
                                         — answers the question "worked *why?*"

   s v

She is taller *than Mary*.

                                  s   v

Word Group: than Mary (is tall — understood) — dependent clause

Function: adverb — modifies the adjective *taller*
                                         — answers the question "*how much* taller?"

  s   v

Patrick swims faster *than Cara*.

                                  s   v

Word Group: than Cara (swims — understood) — dependent clause

Function: adverb — modifies the adverb *faster*
                                       — answers the question "*how much* faster?"

                    s   v

If you are ready, we shall begin the lesson.

                                  s   v

Word Group: If you are ready — dependent clause

Function: adverb — modifies the verb *shall begin*
                                       — answers the question "shall begin *under what condition?*"

WORKING WITH ADVERB CLAUSES

Remember to use the **Test Questions for Adverb Clauses.**

Recognizing

Directions:
1. Identify each verb and its subject in the sentences below.
2. Underline each adverb clause and draw an arrow to the word it modifies.
3. On the line at the left, write the adverb question that the clause answers.

Example: when? After we had eaten breakfast, we visited Mont-Saint-Michel.

_____ 1. The old man walked as if he were tired.

_____ 2. When she entered the room, she noticed the painting.

_____ 3. The woman works where she lives.

_____ 4. The pianist practices so that he can play in the orchestra.

_____ 5. Ellen is happier than Mary.

_____ 6. Richard ran faster than Tim.

_____ 7. Study until you understand the material.

_____ 8. After the surgeon had completed the operation, she called the patient's family.

_____ 9. Because she is happy, she is singing.

_____10. If you are ready now, we shall leave.

BONUS: Tell why there is a comma in the following sentences: #2; #8; #9; and #10.

Composing

Directions: Write one sentence to illustrate each numbered element below. In each sentence identify the verb and its subject; underline the adverb clause and draw an arrow to the word(s) it modifies.

Example: an adverb clause modifying the verb

He jogs <u>because he needs the exercise.</u>

1. an adverb clause answering the question *how?*

2. an adverb clause modifying a predicate adjective

3. an adverb clause answering the question *when?*

4. an adverb clause modifying the verb

5. the adverb clause *than Harry* modifying an adverb

6. an adverb clause answering the question *why?*

7. the adverb clause *when he entered the room* as an introductory adverb clause

8. an adverb clause answering the question *where?*

9. an introductory adverb clause beginning with *if*

10. the adverb clause *than Susan* answering the question *how much happier?*

REVIEWING DEPENDENT CLAUSES

Remembering

Directions: Fill in the blanks with the appropriate words.

1. A dependent clause always contains a _____ and its _____ and expresses an _____ thought.

2. It functions in a sentence as a _____, an _____, or an _____.

3. An introductory adverb clause is usually set off by a _____.

Recognizing

Directions: Underline the dependent clause in each sentence below. If the clause is a noun, write its noun function above it. If it is a modifier, write *adv* or *adj* above it.

1. Give whoever calls, the message.

2. If you are enthusiastic, you will succeed.

3. The film that she most enjoyed was *Citizen Kane*.

4. That this exercise is easy is obvious.

5. He works because he is industrious.

Composing

Directions: Write five consecutive sentences discussing proper study habits. Include in each sentence at least one dependent clause. Underline the clause and write its function above it: noun(s), adv, adj.

BONUS: Extra Credit

Bring to class a recent composition in which you used dependent clauses. Underline the clauses and identify their functions: noun, adv, adj.

THE VERBAL PHRASE

What is a verbal?

A *verbal* is a unique sentence element. It is a *verb form* that usually functions in a sentence as a noun, an adjective, or an adverb. Although a verbal can never function alone as the verb in a clause, it does retain certain verb characteristics: it can have complements and adverb modifiers. There are three types of verbals: *the gerund, the participle, and the infinitive.* (These will be considered separately in the pages that follow.)

What is a verbal phrase?

A verbal phrase is a word group that consists of a verbal and any related complements and modifiers. The three types of verbal phrases are *the gerund phrase, the participial phrase, and the infinitive phrase.*

THE GERUND PHRASE

What is a gerund?

A gerund is a verbal noun. It names an action. It always ends in *ing.*

> *Helping* is a kind act.
> | Gerund: | helping |
> | Function: | noun — subject |

> She was rewarded for *having helped* the children.
> | Gerund: | having helped |
> | Function: | noun — object of preposition *for* |

What is a gerund phrase?

A gerund phrase is a word group consisting of a gerund and any related modifiers and complements. Because a gerund is a *noun*, it can be modified by an adjective. Because a gerund is a *verbal*, it retains verb characteristics: it can have adverbial modifiers and complements.

How can a gerund phrase be identified in a particular sentence?

It can be identified with the **Test Questions for Gerund Phrases.**

TEST QUESTIONS FOR GERUND PHRASES

■ **Does the word group contain a gerund and any related complements and modifiers?**

His encouraging others is his strength.

(with s over *His* and v over *is*)

Gerund Phrase:	His encouraging others
Gerund:	encouraging
Complement:	others — direct object answering the question "encouraging *whom?*"

Note: The complement illustrates a verb characteristic of the gerund.

Modifiers:	His — adjective telling "*whose* encouraging?"

Note: The adjective illustrates a noun characteristic of a gerund: it can be modified by an adjective.

Note: A gerund phrase may contain either a complement or a modifier.

His encouraging is his strength

Gerund Phrase:	His encouraging
Modifier:	His — adjective

Encouraging others is his strength.

Gerund Phrase:	Encouraging others
Complement:	others — direct object

■ Does the word group serve one of the main noun functions?

1. Subject (s)

        s   v
    Studying sentences is enjoyable.

2. Predicate noun (pn)

       s   v   pn
    Her hobby is *studying sentences*.

3. Appositive (app)

       s   app
    Her hobby, *studying sentences*,
    v
    is fun.

4. Direct object (do)

      s v   do
    She likes *studying sentences*.

5. Indirect object (io) rare

      s   v   io
    She gives *studying sentences*
    her reason for success.

6. Object of preposition (op)

      s   v
    She attributes her success in
                 op
    life to *her studying sentences*.

WORKING WITH GERUND PHRASES

Remember to use the **Test Questions for Gerund Phrases.**

Recognizing (Gerunds)

Directions: After identifying the verb and its subject in each sentence, underline each gerund and write its function above it.

Example: <u>Surfing</u> occupies her spare time.

1. Sharing memories is enjoyable.

2. Her hobby is swimming.

3. His favorite pastime is collecting rare stamps.

4. Everyone approves of his studying.

5. They enjoy operating a hotdog stand.

Recognizing (Gerund Phrases)

Directions: After identifying each verb and its subject in the sentences below, underline the gerund phrase and write its function above it.

Example: <u>John's working successfully</u> is obvious.

1. Thinking positively about school is his reason for success.

2. She believes in respecting the opinions of others.

3. Revising a composition is usually necessary.

4. His ambition is writing provocative essays.

5. He enjoys finding unusual essay topics.

6. Her paragraph assignment, developing specific sentences, was productive.

7. Overcoming sentence problems is a worthy goal.

8. Knowing the reasons for classroom assignments is important.

9. She works toward achieving excellence.

10. After completing the assignment, Sara attended a movie.

BONUS: Tell why there is a comma in sentence #10.

Composing

Directions: Write one sentence to illustrate each numbered element that follows. After identifying the verb and its subject in each sentence, underline each gerund phrase and write its function above it.

Example: a gerund phrase as the subject

s   v

Swimming during the summer is her hobby.

1. a gerund phrase as the subject

2. a gerund phrase as a predicate noun

3. a gerund phrase as an appositive

4. a gerund phrase as a direct object

5. a gerund phrase as the object of a preposition

6. a gerund phrase modified by an adjective answering the question *whose?*

7. the gerund phrase *playing the piano* as a direct object

8. the gerund phrase *studying algebra* as the subject

9. the gerund phrase *planning a college career* as the object of the preposition *for*

10. the gerund phrase *opening the vault* as a predicate noun

THE PARTICIPIAL PHRASE

What is a participle?

A participle is a principal part of a verb. Consider the *present* and *past participles* in the chart below.

PRINCIPAL PARTS OF VERB	REGULAR VERB	IRREGULAR VERB
1. present infinitive	walk	run
2. *present participle*	*walking*	*running*
3. past tense	walked	ran
4. *past participle*	*walked*	*run*

Note: If a verb is regular, its past tense and past participle are alike: *walked, walked.*

If a verb is irregular, its past tense and part participle are different: *ran, run.*

A participle can function in two ways.

1. Participle as Part of Verb Phrase
   When a participle combines with a helping verb to form a verb phrase, the participle functions as a verb.

   <blockquote>
   s   v
   The speaker is interesting his listeners.
   </blockquote>

Participle	interesting
Function:	verb — part of verb phrase

2. Participle as Verbal Adjective
   When the participle functions alone in a sentence — not as part of a verb phrase — it is an adjective.

   <blockquote>
   s   v   pa
   The speaker is interesting.
   </blockquote>

Participle:	interesting
Function:	adjective — tells "*what kind of* speaker?"

   <blockquote>
   s   v
   The lost child was found.
   </blockquote>

Participle:	lost
Function:	adjective — tells "*which* child?"

```
┌─────────────────────────────────────────────────────────────────────┐
│                                                                       │
│                   INSTANT CHECK: Participle                           │
│                                                                       │
│  To find whether a word is a participle, test it by checking its      │
│  verb parts.                                                          │
│                 Is the word lost a participle?                        │
│                 Yes: lose, losing, lost, lost                         │
│                                                                       │
└─────────────────────────────────────────────────────────────────────┘
```

What is a participial phrase?

A participial phrase is a word group consisting of a participle (a verbal adjective), and any related complements and modifiers. Remember, because a participle is part verb, it can take complements. A participle can also be modified by adverbs.

How can a participial phrase be identified in a particular sentence?

It can be identified with the **Test Questions for Participial Phrases**.

TEST QUESTIONS FOR PARTICIPIAL PHRASES

■ **Does the word group contain a participle and any related complements and modifiers?**

$$\text{The student } \overset{s}{} \textit{writing a composition} \overset{v}{\text{ works}} \text{ industriously.}$$

The student *writing a composition* works industriously.

Word Group:	writing a composition
Participle:	writing (write, *writing*, wrote, written)
Complement:	composition — direct object answering the question "writing *what?*"

The novel *bound in red leather* is a rare book.

Word Group:	bound in red leather
Participle:	bound (bind, binding, bound, *bound*)
Modifier:	in red leather — adverb telling "*how* bound?"

64

■ Does the word group function as an adjective?

                            s   v

The student *writing a composition* works industriously.

Word Group:	writing a composition — participial phrase
Function:	adjective — modifies the noun *student*
	— tells "*which* student?"

INSTANT CHECK: Participle or Gerund?

Note: Both gerunds and present participles end in *ing*. The only way to distinguish between them is to check their sentence functions. Consider the following phrases:

    Running in the corridor, the student fell.

Word Group	Running in the corridor
Function:	adjective modifying the subject
	student — participial phrase

    Running in the corridor is unsafe.

Word Group:	Running in the corridor
Function:	subject of sentence answering the question "*what* is unsafe?" — gerund phrase

---

WORKING WITH PARTICIPIAL PHRASES

Remember to use the **Test Questions for Participial Phrases**.

Recognizing (Participles)

Directions: After identifying the verb and its subject, underline the participle in each sentence below and draw an arrow to the word it modifies. To be sure the word is a participle, write the four principal parts of the verb represented on the line below and circle the participle used.

Example: Running in the corridor, the student fell.

run (running) ran run

1. The small child sitting near the window seems lonely.

_____ _____ _____ _____

2. Vegetables planted in fertile soil grow well.

_____ _____ _____ _____

3. Arriving before the conference, the lecturer waited impatiently.

_____ _____ _____ _____

4. He is the person appointed for the position.

_____ _____ _____ _____

5. Listening carefully, she gazed into the darkness.

_____ _____ _____ _____

Recognizing (Participial Phrases)

Directions: After identifying the verb and its subject, underline each participial phrase and draw an arrow to the word it modifies.

Example: Running in the corridor, she slipped.

1. The young woman, appreciating the flowers, smiled happily.

2. The novel *Huckleberry Finn*, now studied in many literature courses, was praised by Ernest Hemingway.

3. Encouraged by her enthusiasm, the actor continued with the story.

4. Studying in the library, Hans concentrated on his history assignment.

5. The conference held in Paris was an international success.

6. Outlining his composition, Phil checked for effective parallel structure.

7. The young skier, enjoying his favorite sport, careened down the trail.

8. Relying upon his wit, Odysseus outsmarted the Cyclopes.

9. The old woman lost in her memories did not hear the young woman.

10. A composition written well impresses the reader.

BONUS: Explain the commas in sentences #3, #4, and #8.

Composing

Directions: Write one sentence to illustrate each numbered element that follows. Identify the verb and its subject. Underline each participial phrase and draw an arrow to the word it modifies.

Example: The participial phrase *sitting in the corner* modifying the direct object.

```
s   v      do
I saw the boy sitting in the corner.
```

1. a participial phrase modifying the subject

2. the introductory participial phrase *running in the corridor* modifying the subject *child*

3. the participial phrase *lost in the woods* modifying a predicate noun

4. a participial phrase modifying a direct object

5. a participial phrase modifying the subject *teacher*

6. the participial phrase *sitting near me* modifying the direct object

7. a participial phrase modifying the object of a preposition

8. the participial phrase *approaching me* modifying the subject

9. a participial phrase modifying a predicate noun

10. the participial phrase *sold to the stranger* modifying the word *antique*

THE INFINITIVE PHRASE

What is an infinitive?

An infinitive is a verb form usually consisting of the word *to* and a verb. The word *to* is called the sign of the infinitive. An infinitive functions in a sentence as a noun, an adjective, or an adverb.

     S   V
To succeed is rewarding.

    Infinitive: To succeed

    Function: noun — subject

   S V
This is the time *to work*.

    Infinitive: to work

    Function: adjective — answers the question "*which* time?"

   S V
He studied *to learn*.

    Infinitive: to learn

    Function: adverb — answers the question "studied *why*?"

   Note: Sometimes the sign of the infinitive *to* is omitted.
     Please let me *go* skiing.
      Infinitive: go
      Sign: to — not expressed
     Permit me *to go* skiing.
      Infinitive: to go
      Sign: to — expressed

What is an infinitive phrase?

An infinitive phrase is a word group consisting of an infinitive and any related complements and modifiers. Because an infinitive is part verb, it can have complements and adverb modifiers.

How can an infinitive phrase be identified in a particular sentence?

It can be identified with the **Test Questions for Infinitive Phrases.**

TEST QUESTIONS FOR INFINITIVE PHRASES

■ **Does the word group contain an infinitive and any related complements and modifiers?**

To develop confidence is her ambition.

Word Group:	To develop confidence
Infinitive:	To develop
Complement:	confidence — direct object answering the question "to develop *what?*"

He wants *to be happy*.

Word Group:	to be happy
Infinitive:	to be
Complement:	happy — adjective modifying the subject *he*

To work quickly is productive.

Word Group:	To work quickly
Infinitive:	To work
Modifier:	quickly — adverb answering the question "to work *how?*"

■ **Does the word group function in the sentence as a noun?**

subject (s)

$$\overset{s}{\text{To understand this lesson}} \overset{v}{\text{is}} \text{ essential.}$$

predicate noun (pn)

$$\overset{s}{\text{The object}} \overset{v}{\text{is}} \overset{pn}{\textit{to understand this lesson.}}$$

appositive (app)

$$\overset{s}{\text{His goal}}, \overset{app}{\textit{to attend college}}, \overset{v}{\text{has become}} \text{ a reality.}$$

direct object (do)

$$\overset{s}{\text{She}} \overset{v}{\text{wants}} \overset{do}{\textit{to be an engineer.}}$$

■ **Does the word group function in the sentence as an adjective?**

The car *to buy now* is a Ford.

Word Group:	to buy now — infinitive phrase
Function:	adjective — answers the question "*which* car?"

■ **Does the word group function as an adverb?**

The passenger ran *to catch the bus.*

Word Group:	to catch the bus — infinitive phrase
Function:	adverb — answers the question "ran *why?*"

WORKING WITH INFINITIVE PHRASES

Remember to use the **Test Questions for Infinitive Phrases**.

Recognizing (Infinitives)

Directions: After identifying the verb and its subject in each sentence below, underline each infinitive and write its function above it: n (noun); adj (adjective); or adv (adverb).

n-s   v
Example: <u>To work</u> is a privilege.

1. Henry likes to ice-skate.

2. Sheila has permission to go.

3. Paul studies to succeed.

4. To play the piano well is a great pleasure.

5. Her desire is to travel.

Recognizing (Infinitive Phrases)

Directions: After identifying the verb and its subject in each sentence below, underline each infinitive phrase and write its function above it. If it is a modifier, write *adj* or *adv* and draw an arrow from the modifier to the word modified. If it is a noun, write its function: s, pn, app, do, io, op.

s   v   adv
Examples: He worked <u>to attend college</u>.

s   v   adj
She has permission <u>to attend the lecture</u>.

s   v   do
They like <u>to travel in Europe</u>.

1. She worked to earn money for college.

2. To baffle the audience, the magician performed another trick.

3. To baffle the audience is the magician's challenge.

4. The farmer intends to harvest his corn tomorrow.

5. The book to read first is the instruction manual.

6. To work quietly is necessary, for the library is crowded.

7. She ran to catch the early bus.

8. He wanted to travel in Spain.

9. Tina hopes to fly to Italy to visit her grandparents.

10. His goal is to study in London.

11. She searched to find the key.

Composing

Directions: Write one sentence to illustrate each numbered element that follows. Identify the verb and its subject. Underline each infinitive phrase. If the phrase is a modifier, write *adj* or *adv* above it, and draw an arrow to the word it modifies. If the phrase is a noun, write its noun function above it.

Example: an infinitive phrase as direct object

    s   v   do
He wants <u>to learn Russian</u>.

1. an infinitive phrase as the subject

2. an infinitive phrase as an adjective modifying the direct object *permission*

3. an infinitive phrase as a direct object

4. an infinitive phrase as an adverb modifying the predicate adjective *happy*

5. the infinitive phrase *to please everyone* as a predicate noun

6. the infinitive phrase *to read novels* as the subject

7. an introductory infinitive phrase modifying the subject

8. the infinitive phrase *to appreciate literature* as a direct object

9. an infinitive phrase as an adverb answering the question *why?*

10. an infinitive phrase as an adjective answering the question *what kind of?*

INTRODUCTORY VERBAL PHRASES

What is an introductory verbal phrase?

It is a gerund phrase, a participial phrase,or an infinitive phrase that precedes the subject of the sentence and always *refers* to the subject.

Examples:

                                s   v
— On *entering the room*, I saw my friend.

         Introductory Form: entering the room — gerund phrase

         Function: object of the preposition *on*

                       Note: The entire prepositional phrase (on entering the room) precedes the subject *I* and refers to it.

                           s   v
— *Entering the room*, I saw my friend.

         Introductory Form: Entering the room — participial phrase

         Function: adjective modifying the subject *I* which it precedes.

                           s   v
— *To reach the airport on time*, she drove quickly through the traffic.

         Introductory Form: To reach the airport quickly — infinitive phrase

         Function: modifier that refers to the subject *she*.

How is any introductory verbal phrase punctuated?

It is always followed by a *comma*.

WORKING WITH INTRODUCTORY VERBAL PHRASES

Recognizing

Directions: The sentences that follow contain introductory verbal phrases. Punctuate each phrase correctly, underline it, and identify its type: g (gerund); p (participial); i (infinitive).

Example: Walking in the department store I fell.

p
<u>Walking in the department store</u>, I fell.

1. To be successful in my geometry class I must prepare my homework.

2. Running in the gym Terri sprained her ankle.

3. On entering the classroom Sheila found her chemistry book.

4. Exhausted by the weekend parties Jack fell asleep in class.

5. To ride a horse gracefully a person must practice frequently.

Composing

Directions: Write three sentences. In the first include an introductory gerund phrase; in the second, include an introductory participial phrase; in the third, include an introductory infinitive phrase. Punctuate each sentence correctly. Underline the phrase and identify its type by placing the letter g, p, or i above it.

REVIEWING VERBAL PHRASES

Remembering Verbals

Directions: Fill in the blanks with the appropriate words.

1. A verbal is a _____ form used as another part of speech.

2. There are three types of verbals: the gerund which functions as a _____; the participle which functions as an _____; and the infinitive which functions as a _____, an _____ or an _____.

BONUS: Extra Credit
Verbals

Complete the following analogies.

a. *ing* : gerund :: _____ : infinitive

b. gerund : noun :: participle : _____

c. participle : noun :: infinitive : verb or preposition

Complete the following blanks with the term *gerund*, *infinitive*, or *participle*.

a. Always a noun _____

   Never a noun _____

   Sometimes a noun _____

b. Always an adjective _____

   Never an adjective _____

   Sometimes an adjective _____

c. Always ends in *ing* _____

   Never ends in *ing* _____

   Sometimes ends in *ing* _____

Remembering Verbal Phrases

Directions: Fill in the blanks with the appropriate words.

1. A verbal phrase consists of a verbal and any related _____ or _____.

2. There are three types of verbal phrases: the gerund phrase which always functions as a _____; the participial phrase which functions as an _____; and the infinitive phrase which may function as a noun, an adjective or an _____.

3. An introductory verbal phrase precedes the _____ of the sentence. It is always followed by a _____.

Recognizing

Directions: Each sentence that follows contains one verbal phrase.
Circle its type: g (gerund); p (participle); i (infinitive).

1. She is the girl holding the book.   g, p, i

2. His object is to succeed in sports. g, p, i

3. Her hobby, collecting stamps, occupies her free time.   g, p, i

4. To catch the bus, she ran swiftly.   g, p, i

5. Leaving the room, he slipped and fell.   g, p, i

BONUS: Explain the use of a comma in sentence #4 and in sentence #5.

Composing

Directions: Write one sentence to illustrate each numbered element below. Punctuate each sentence correctly.

1. *to study carefully* as an introductory infinitive phrase

2. *entering the room* as an introductory gerund phrase that is the object of the preposition *on*

3. *rushing into the room* as an introductory participial phrase

BONUS: Extra Credit
Verbal Phrases

Bring to class a recent composition in which you used verbal phrases. Underline each phrase and identify it according to type: g, p, i. Especially note (*) any introductory phrases.

REVIEW OF MAJOR FUNCTIONS AND FORMS

What then are the major sentence functions?

They are the *verb*, the *noun*, the *adjective*, and the *adverb*.

What are the major forms?

They are the *dependent clause* and the *verbal phrase*.

How do the functions and forms relate in the sentence?

Any major *form* always *functions* as a noun, an adjective, or an adverb. See the chart that follows:

CHART OF RELATED MAJOR FUNCTIONS AND FORMS

Sentence: The *verb* is its heart. (Complete Thought)

Form	Function
Dependent Clause	
(Incomplete Thought)	
Noun Clause	Noun
Adjective Clause	Adjective
Adverb Clause	Adverb
Verbal Phrase	
Gerund Phrase	Noun
Participial Phrase	Adjective
Infinitive Phrase	Noun Adjective Adverb

REVIEW PROCEDURE FOR SENTENCE ANALYSIS

What then, in review, is the procedure for sentence analysis?

The procedure is *to ask* the right questions to identify the following:

1. **The verb** (action or linking)
   Word
   Phrase (verb phrase)

2. **The subject**
   Word
   Phrase (gerund phrase or infinitive phrase)
   Clause (noun clause)

3. **Any complements:** direct object, indirect object, predicate noun, (predicate adjective — see modifiers.)
   Word
   Phrase (gerund phrase or infinitive phrase)
   Clause (noun clause)

4. **Any modifiers:** adjective or adverb
   Word
   Phrase (prepositional, infinitive) + participial for adjective only
   Clause (adjective or adverb)

Note: The other noun functions, the appositive and the object of the preposition can be word, phrase, or clause.

What does the "Review Procedure for Sentence Analysis" demonstrate about sentences?

It demonstrates that sentences contain the same basic parts: the *verb*; its *subject*; any related *complements*; any related *modifiers*.

— These parts represent specific sentence *functions* that take various sentence *forms*: word, phrase, clause.

— Sentences contain, therefore, the interrelating functions and forms.

How does knowledge of sentence functions and forms prepare students for their forthcoming study of sentence usage?

Since sentence usage concerns the "proper" and "improper" relationships of the *functions* and *forms*, students should realize that they already have the necessary knowledge for understanding sentence usage and for improving sentences.

PART III — SENTENCE USAGE

To understand sentence usage, students must know the relationship between grammatical principles and the application of these principles in sentences.

Accepted sentence usage represents the "proper" use of the interrelating sentence functions and forms.

The function determines the form.

Unaccepted sentence usage represents the "misuse" of the interrelating sentence functions and forms.

The form used is incorrect for the function intended.

Purpose

Part III shows students how to apply their grammatical knowledge of function and form so that they can understand the basis of accepted and unaccepted usage and eliminate the unaccepted forms, the 'common errors' in English, from their own sentences.

Approach

This section builds upon the "Outline of Common Errors" compiled by Earl Wood in the *Junior English Review Exercises* and the *Senior English Review Exercises.** It provides the grammatical foundation for understanding these errors by demonstrating the following:

— the grammatical principle related to each error

— the problem that results from the improper application of this principle

— the grammatical explanation of **why** each error is considered an error

— the method(s) of correcting each error

It also provides many opportunities for proofreading practice.

Sequence

Repetition with understanding is the key to using this approach successfully. Thus the approach is sequential and cumulative. Students should **strive to understand these principles and their applications**, not merely to memorize sentence patterns.

Positive Results

Experience has proved that students who use this system with understanding will not only eliminate these errors from their writing but also use grammatical forms effectively to improve their writing styles.

Note: This section is used most effectively in conjunction with a consistent composition program. Students must experience frequent opportunities to see and to use the forms and functions in their own compositions. The section "Bonus Activities for A—P" offers some suggestions for related writing exercises.

* Available from Educators Publishing Service, Cambridge, Mass.

A. LACK OF PARALLELISM Proofreading Symbol: //

PARALLELISM

Principle: Sentence elements alike in function should be alike in form. Like elements are usually joined by the coordinate conjunctions (+) *and, but, or, nor, for.*

Problem: Sentence elements alike in function are unlike in form.
Clue: The coordinate conjunction (+).

A1. INFINITIVE-GERUND

INCORRECT

```
s   v   do  +   do
```
She likes *to ski* and *swimming.*

> **Unlike Forms:** *to ski* — infinitive
> *swimming* — gerund

> **Like Functions:** direct objects — Both italicized forms answer the question "likes *what*?"

> **Remember:** *Sentence elements alike in function should be alike in form.*
> Study, therefore, the correct examples.

CORRECT

```
s   v   do  +   do
```
She likes *to ski* and *to swim.*

> **Like Forms:** *to ski* — infinitive
> *to swim* — infinitive

> **Like Functions:** direct objects

or

```
s   v   do  +   do
```
She likes *skiing* and *swimming.*

> **Like Forms:** *skiing* — gerund
> *swimming* — gerund

> **Like Functions:** direct objects

83

A2. PHRASE — CLAUSE

INCORRECT

<pre>
 s   v   adv   +   adv
Paul will win <i>because of his persistence</i> and <i>because he is intelligent</i>.
</pre>

Unlike Forms: *because of his persistence* — phrase
because he is intelligent — clause

Like Functions: adverbs — Both italicized word groups modify the verb
will win and answer the question "will win *why?*"

Remember: ***Sentence elements alike in function should be alike in form.***
Study, therefore, the correct examples.

CORRECT

<pre>
 s   v   op   +   op
Paul will win because of his <i>persistence</i> and <i>intelligence</i>.
</pre>

Like Forms: *persistence* — word
intelligence — word

Like Functions: objects of the preposition *because of*

or

<pre>
 s   v   pa   +   pa
Paul will win because he is <i>persistent</i> and <i>intelligent</i>.
</pre>

Like Forms: *persistent* — word
intelligent — word

Like Functions: predicate adjectives — both words modify *he*, the subject
of the clause.

Now each coordinate conjunction (+) joins elements that are equal in
function and form.

A3. MISPLACED CORRELATIVES

Rule: Correlatives are coordinate conjunctions that are used in pairs: *either — or; neither — nor; both — and; not only — but also.* Correlative conjunctions join elements that are equal in function and form.

INCORRECT

<pre>
    s   v   pa   adv   adv
The athlete is <i>not only</i> popular in Maine <i>but also</i> in California.
</pre>

In the above example the correlatives are placed before elements unlike in form and function.

Correlative	Placed Before	Form/Function
not only	popular	Form: word Function: predicate adjective
but also	in California	Form: phrase Function: adverb

CORRECT

<pre>
    s   v   pa   adv   adv
The athlete is popular <i>not only</i> in Maine <i>but also</i> in California.
</pre>

Now the correlatives are placed before elements equal in form and function.

Like Forms: in Maine — phrase
                in California — phrase

Like Functions: adverbs — both phrases tell "*where* popular?"

A4. UNNECESSARY SHIFT IN PERSON AND VOICE

REVIEW: Person and Voice

(Form changes in *Pronoun* and *Verb*)

Person: (Pronoun)	First Person	speaker	I, we
	Second Person	person spoken to	you
	Third Person	person spoken about	he, she, it, they

Voice: (Verb)	Active Voice (Subject acts)	He *hits* the ball.
	Passive Voice (Subject is acted upon)	He *was hit* by the ball.

Note: A passive verb is always a *verb phrase*.

Formula: A passive verb = a form of the verb *to be* as the helping verb + the past participle of the main verb.*

* See *Appendix B* for information on principal parts of verbs.

INCORRECT

s   v   +   s   v

Yesterday *I studied* Spanish and then *television was watched* by me.

> The coordinate conjunction joins two independent clauses; the subject and verb in each clause are unnecessarily different.

Unlike Forms: *I studied*
s v
Verb: *studied* — active voice
Subject: *I* — first person singular

television was watched
s   v
Verb: *was watched* — passive voice
Subject: *television* — third person singular

Like Functions: Both word groups function as independent clauses in the same sentence.

CORRECT

$$\overset{\text{s}\quad\text{v}}{\text{Yesterday } \textit{I studied} \text{ Spanish}} \quad + \quad \overset{\text{s}\quad\text{v}}{\text{then } \textit{I watched} \text{ television.}}$$

s v + s v
Yesterday *I studied* Spanish and then *I watched* television.

Now the coordinate conjunction joins elements that are equal.

Like Forms:
s v
I studied
Verb: *studied* — active voice
Subject: *I* — first person singular

s v
I watched
Verb: *watched* — active voice
Subject: *I* — first person singular

Like Functions: Both word groups function as independent clauses in the same sentence.

A5. IMPROPER SERIES

INCORRECT

s v 1. pa 2. pa + 3. pa
The student is *conscientious, energetic,* and *she is also competent.*

Series: three or more items.

Unlike Forms: *conscientious* — word
energetic — word
she is also competent — clause

Like Functions: predicate adjectives

Note: The clause stresses the predicate adjective *competent.*

CORRECT

1. pa 2. pa 3. pa
The student is *conscientious, energetic,* and *competent.*

Like Forms: *conscientious* — word
energetic — word
competent — word

Like Functions: predicate adjectives

Proofreading for (A) Errors
Lack of Parallelism (//)

With the aid of the chart below, identify the errors in the sentences that follow. Any sentence that is incorrect contains no more than one error. Write both the letter and the number for all answers except (F).

A1 — infinitive-gerund
A2 — phrase-clause
A3 — misplaced correlatives

A4 — unnecessary shift — person and voice
A5 — improper series
F — correct sentence

(#1)

1. I not only enjoyed the plot of the new science fiction thriller but also the vivid illustrations. _____

2. They plan to purchase the property first and then building condominiums on it. _____

3. Because of her ambition and because she is extremely interested in nutrition, June attended an international institute for nutritional advancement in London. _____

4. The judge insisted that either he return the stolen goods or make restitution for them. _____

5. The English assignments that Marlene enjoys most are reading English novels and then to watch current films. _____

6. In our class on word study, we first studied analogies and then malapropisms were enjoyed by us. _____

7. To study astronomy and traveling in Africa are his main goals. _____

8. The students not only studied antonyms but also synonyms for the English proficiency test. _____

9. We found the vocabulary text exciting, thought-provoking, and it was also brief. _____

10. Linda learned that words like *abbreviate* and *abridge* are doublets, and then Greek derivatives were studied by her. _____

88

Proofreading for (A) Errors

1. We decided to remain in New York because of the fog and because it was raining. ——

2. Either you must finish the sculpture or discard the clay. ——

3. You must not only overcome those difficulties but also master this technique. ——

4. In the morning the athlete wanted to jog along the beach and then exercising in the gymnasium. ——

5. They liked to wander along the seashore and picnicking in the cove. ——

6. The teacher asked us to distinguish between *fragrance* and *odor* and then sentences were written by us. ——

7. The student leader was assertive, affirmative, and she was also charming. ——

8. The philosopher liked to live fully and enjoying his ephemeral existence. ——

9. He always seemed happy because of his sense of humor and because he laughed frequently. ——

10. They wanted not only to emulate famous people but also to follow their peers. ——

BONUS: Parallelism

Write a parody of a famous speech that employs effective parallel structure. (If the speech is long, write a parody of an excerpt from such a speech.) Be sure to use parallel structure in your own version.

For example: Write a parody of Lincoln's Gettysburg Address or of Kennedy's Inaugural Address.

CASE

Principle: The case or *form* of a noun or pronoun is determined by the *function* of the noun or pronoun in a particular sentence.

Problem: The wrong case is used for the function that is indicated.

B1 – B6 CASE

The three case forms in English are the *nominative*, the *objective*, and the *possessive*. Note: The relationship between the noun (pronoun) functions and the case forms is as follows:

Noun-Pronoun Functions

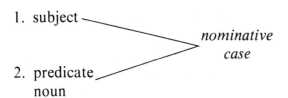

1. subject
2. predicate noun
              nominative case
3. appositive   case of the noun or pronoun renamed

4. direct object
5. indirect object ———→ *objective case*
6. object of the preposition

Usual Pronoun (Noun) Functions and Forms

The change in case is evident primarily in pronouns. Noun changes are evident in the possessive case.

Function: subject (s); predicate noun (pn)
Form: *Nominative Case*
          I, you, he, she, it — singular
          we, you, they — plural
          who, whoever

Function: direct object (do); indirect object (io); object of preposition (op)
Form: *Objective Case*
          me, you him, her, it — singular
          us, you, them — plural
          whom, whomever

Function: usually adjective answering the question "whose?"
Form: *Possessive Case*

my, mine, your, yours, his, her, hers, its
our, ours, your, yours, their, theirs
whose
Mary's, Charles's, Burns'

Note: The apostrophe is not used on possessive pronouns.

B1. BEFORE A GERUND

Rule: Use the possessive case of a noun or pronoun before a gerund.

INCORRECT

```
          s        v           gerund
```
The teacher disapproves of *him* studying in the recreation area.

> **Form Used:** *him* — objective case

> **Function Indicated:** possessive adjective — answering the question "*whose* studying?" — possessive case

Note: The teacher approves of him.

but

The teacher disapproves of his action, studying in the recreation area.

CORRECT

```
          s        v           gerund
```
The teacher disapproves of *his* studying in the recreation area.

> Now form and function agree.

> **Form:** *his* — possessive case

> **Function:** possessive adjective answering the question "*whose* studying?" — possessive case

91

B2. PREDICATE PRONOUN AFTER A LINKING VERB

Rule: Use the same case after the linking verb as the case of the noun or pronoun renamed. (Remember: The verb *to be* is like an equal sign.)

INCORRECT

        s   v pn
The detective is *him*, the man approaching the warehouse.
        (=)

      Form Used: *him* — objective case

      Function Indicated: predicate pronoun (pn) — renaming the subject
                  detective which is nominative case

CORRECT

        s   v pn
The detective is *he*, the man approaching the warehouse.
        (=)

      Now form and function agree.

      Form: *he* — nominative case

      Function: predicate pronoun (pn) renaming nominative subject *detective*
               (*he*, nominative case = *detective*, nominative case)

INCORRECT

s   v   pn
It certainly must have been *her*.
             (=)

      Form Used: *her* — objective case

      Function Indicated: predicate pronoun (pn) renaming the nominative
               subject *It*

CORRECT

```
s                v     pn
It certainly must have been she.
                   (=)
```

Now form and function agree.

Form: *she* — nominative case

Function: predicate pronoun renaming nominative subject *It*
(*she*, nominative case = *it*, nominative case)

B3. SUBJECT OF AN INFINITIVE

Rule: The subject of an infinitive is in the objective case.

INCORRECT

```
s    v (s of inf)
We know she to be the principal.
           (=)
```

Form Used: *she* — nominative case

Function Indicated: subject of the infinitive *to be*, objective case

CORRECT

```
s    v (s of inf)
We know her to be the principal.
           (=)
```

Now form and function agree.

Form: *her* — objective case

Function: subject of the infinitive, objective case

Note: Do not confuse the subject of the infinitive with the direct object. In the above example the entire infinitive phrase *her to be the principal* functions as the direct object. The phrase expresses an idea similar to that of a noun clause:

```
s v       noun clause—d.o.
I know that she is the principal.
```

93

B4. PREDICATE PRONOUN AFTER AN INFINITIVE

Rule: A predicate pronoun (pn) takes the same case as the noun or pronoun it renames. (Only a linking verb can take a pn)

INCORRECT

```
 s      v      (s of inf)      pn
```
We know the principal to be *she*.

> **Form Used:** *she* — nominative case

> **Function Indicated:** predicate pronoun renaming the subject of the infinitive *principal*, objective case

CORRECT

```
 s      v      (s of inf)      pn
```
We know the principal to be *her*.

> Now form and function agree.

> **Form:** *her* — objective case

> **Function:** predicate pronoun renaming *principal*, subject of the infinitive and objective case
> *her*, objective case = *principal*, objective case

B5. DIRECT OBJECT AFTER A VERB (PHRASE) OR VERBAL

Rule: A direct object takes the objective case.

INCORRECT

```
      s      v      do  +  do
```
The coach invited Paul and *I* to the game.

> **Form Used:** *I* — nominative case

> **Function Indicated:** a direct object of the verb *invited* answering the question "invited *whom*?"

94

Note: Testmakers trick students with the sound of expressions such as *Paul and me*. (Most students would not say, "The coach invited *I* to the game.")

CORRECT

<pre>
     s   v   do + do
</pre>
The coach invited Paul and *me* to the game.

Now form and function agree

Form: *me* — objective case

Function: direct object, objective case

INCORRECT

Who are you willing to nominate?

<pre>
   s   v   inf   do
</pre>
You are willing to nominate *who*?

Form Used: *who* — nominative case

Function Indicated: direct object of the infinitive, objective case

CORRECT

<pre>
    do   s   inf
</pre>
Whom are you willing to nominate?

Now form and function agree.

Form: *whom* — objective case

Function: direct object of the infinitive *to nominate*, objective case

B6. OBJECT OF A PREPOSITION

Rule: The object of a preposition takes the objective case.

INCORRECT

```
s      p     op   +   op   v
```
All except Kerry and *we* are attending the concert.

> **Form Used:** *we* — nominative case

> **Function Indicated:** object of the preposition *except*, objective case

CORRECT

```
s      p     op   +   op   v
```
All except Kerry and *us* are attending the concert.

> Now form and function agree.

> **Form:** *us* — objective case

> **Function:** object of the preposition, objective case

Proofreading for (B) Errors
Improper Case: (ca)

With the aid of the chart below, identify the errors in the sentences that follow. Any sentence that is incorrect contains no more than one error. Write both the letter and the number for all answers except (F):

B1 — before a gerund
B2 — predicate pronoun after a linking verb
B3 — subject of an infinitive
B4 — predicate pronoun after an infinitive

B5 — direct object after a verb (phrase) or verbal
B6 — object of a preposition
F — correct sentence

(#1)

1. The principal approves of us attending the state championship game. ‗‗‗

2. Are you planning to invite him to the party? ‗‗‗

3. The Olympic gold-medal winner is her, the woman approaching the stadium. ‗‗‗

4. We know she to be the silver-medal winner of the ten-meter platform dive. ‗‗‗

5. All but Alec and he participated in the diving competition. ‗‗‗

6. I should like to be she. ‗‗‗

7. Who are you going to invite to the play? ‗‗‗

8. Her brother is the person who invited us to the basketball game. ‗‗‗

9. The teacher is her. ‗‗‗

10. I know her to be the celebrity. ‗‗‗

Proofreading for (B) Errors

(#2)

1. Louise knew the acrobat to be him. ‗‗‗

2. The octogenarian is him, the old man scuffling toward us. ‗‗‗

3. The alleged thief knew the law officer to be she. ‗‗‗

4. Father gave the car keys to Bob and I. ‗‗‗

97

5. Everybody is pleased at Judy winning a scholarship at Dartmouth. _____

6. They wanted to call Dr. Norton whom they knew to be the leading heart specialist. _____

7. The talk show hostess is her, the person who is enthusiastic, attentive, and intelligent. _____

8. The teacher disapproves of us leaving our notebooks and pens in our lockers. _____

9. The comic would like to be he. _____

10. We knew she to be the social worker. _____

Proofreading for (A) and (B) Errors
Lack of Parallelism (//); Improper Case (ca)

With the aid of the chart below, identify the errors in the sentences that follow. Any sentence that is incorrect contains no more than one error. Write both the letter and the number for all answers except (F).

(A) — lack of parallelism
A1 — infinitive-gerund
A2 — phrase-clause
A3 — misplaced correlatives
A4 — unnecessary shift person and voice
A5 — improper series
(B) — improper case
B1 — before a gerund

B2 — predicate pronoun after a linking verb
B3 — subject of an infinitive
B4 — predicate pronoun after an infinitive
B5 — direct object after a verb (phrase) or verbal
B6 — object of a preposition
F — correct sentence

1. Philip will leave because of his fatigue and because he is bored. ____

2. They knew she to be the new physics instructor. ____

3. He not only refused to study French but also to write compositions. ____

4. A successful statesman must study, concentrate, and then to perform well. ____

5. Mother does not approve of Mary working at a resort. ____

6. I should like to be her. ____

7. His architect is she, the person standing on the corner. ____

8. Yesterday I studied for some time and then a good novel was read by me. ____

9. The teacher asked John and I to give oral reports. ____

10. Please give the tickets to Frank and he. ____

C. LACK OF AGREEMENT (Subject — Verb)

AGREEMENT OF SUBJECT AND VERB

Principle: A verb agrees with its subject in number and in person.

Agreement in Number (singular or plural)

        s v
The boy runs.   Subject: *boy*   singular
                                   Verb Form: *runs*

        s v
The boys run.   Subject: *boys*   plural
                                   Verb Form: *run*

Agreement in Person (first, second, or third)

s v
I run   Subject: *I*   first person
                                   Verb Form: *run*

s v
He runs.   Subject: *He*   third person
                                   Verb Form: *runs*

Problem: The wrong form of the verb is used for the stated subject.

C1. VERB AFTER A PREPOSITIONAL PHRASE

Rule: The verb agrees with its subject, not with the object(s) of a preposition.

INCORRECT

                           s   v
The computer's *response* to the operator's many questions *were* very rapid.

        Form Used: *were* — plural

        Function Indicated: agreement with singular subject *response*, not
                                    with the plural object of the preposition, *questions*

CORRECT

	s	v

The computer's *response* to the operator's many questions *was* very rapid.

> **Form:** *was* — singular

> **Function:** agreement in number with the singular subject *response*

INCORRECT

The *results* of his answer *affects* all of us.

> **Form Used:** *affects* — singular

> **Function Indicated:** agreement with the plural subject *results*, not with the singular object *answer*

CORRECT

The *results* of his answer *affect* all of us.

> **Form:** *affect* — plural

> **Function:** agreement with plural subject *results*

C2. VERB IN A DEPENDENT CLAUSE

Rule: The verb in a dependent clause agrees with the subject of its clause.

INCORRECT

Alice is one of those students *who* always *receives* an 'A'.

> **Form Used:** *receives* — singular

> **Function Indicated:** agreement with its subject *who*, which is plural. The pronoun *who* refers to its plural antecedent *students*. *Of those students* who always receive an 'A', Alice is one.

Note: She is not the *only one*. She is part of a group.

CORRECT

$\overset{\text{s}}{}\qquad\overset{\text{v}}{}$

Alice is one of those students *who* always *receive* an 'A'.

Now form agrees with function.

Form: *receive* — plural

Function: agreement with the plural subject *who*

C3. VERB AFTER AN EXPLETIVE

Rule: The verb should agree with its subject, not with an expletive, an introductory word such as *it* or *there.*

INCORRECT

exp   v   s
There *seems* to be several *chocolates* missing.

Form Used: *seems* — singular

Function Indicated: agreement with the plural subject *chocolates*, answering the question "*what* seems?" not with the expletive *there*

CORRECT

exp   v   s
There *seem* to be several *chocolates* missing.

Now form agrees with function.

Form: *seem* — plural

Function: agreement with plural subject *chocolates*

C4. VERB WITH AN INDEFINITE PRONOUN

Rule: Certain indefinite pronouns take singular verb forms. (*Each one, every one, each, either, neither, one, no one, etc.*)

INCORRECT

s   v

Each one of the students *are* requested to report at noon.

> **Form Used:** *are requested* — plural

> **Function Indicated:** agreement with the singular subject *each one*

CORRECT

s   v

Each one of the students *is* requested to report at noon.

> Now form agrees with function.

> **Form:** *is* — singular

> **Function:** agreement with singular subject *each one*

C5. VERB WITH A COLLECTIVE NOUN

> **Rule:** A verb used with a collective noun, the name of a group, is singular when the group is regarded as a unit: clues — *agree, unanimous, its.*
> A verb used with a collective noun is plural when the group members are regarded as individuals: clues — *disagree, their.*

INCORRECT

s   v

The *class have* reached a unanimous decision.

> **Form Used:** *have* — plural

> **Function Indicated:** agreement with the singular subject *class* (clue: *unanimous*)

CORRECT

s   v

The *class has* reached a unanimous decision.

> **Form:** *has* — singular

> **Function:** agreement with the singular subject *class*

Proofreading for (C) Errors
Lack of Agreement-Subject and Verb (agr)

With the aid of the chart below, identify the errors in the sentences that follow. Any sentence that is incorrect contains no more than one error. Write both the letter and the number for all answers except (F).

C1 — verb after a prepositional phrase
C2 — verb in a dependent clause
C3 — verb after an expletive

C4 — verb with an indefinite pronoun
C5 — verb with a collective noun
F — correct sentence

1. Kathy is one of those students who always receives an 'A'. ____

2. There seems to be several students absent today. ____

3. The author's wide interests in literature, education, natural history, and politics proves his versatility. ____

4. Each one present are requested to attend the preliminary conference. ____

5. The committee are about to announce its unanimous decision. ____

6. The poetry collection with its many poems have been donated to the literary society. ____

7. Frank is one of those citizens who always attends town meetings. ____

8. Everybody knows that we will win. ____

9. There definitely seems to be fewer errors in your composition. ____

10. The study of literature and history occupy her spare time. ____

D. LACK OF AGREEMENT (Pronoun and Antecedent)

AGREEMENT OF PRONOUN AND ANTECEDENT

Principle: A pronoun agrees with its antecedent, the noun for which it stands, in person, number, and gender.

Agreement in Person, Number, and Gender

      s   v
Mary expressed *her* opinions.

        Antecedent: *Mary*
                      person: third
                      number: singular
                      gender: feminine

        Pronoun: *her*
                      person: third
                      number: singular
                      gender: feminine

Problem: The pronoun form used disagrees with its stated antecedent in person, number, or gender.

INCORRECT

      s   v   pro
Everyone is writing *their* composition.

        Form Used: *their* — plural pronoun

        Function Indicated: agreement with singular antecedent *everyone*

        Note: Certain indefinite pronouns such as *each, either, neither, everybody, everyone, one, each one,* are singular in number.

CORRECT

      s   v   pro
Everyone is writing *his (her)* composition.

        Form: *his* — singular pronoun, masculine gender

Note: Traditionally the masculine form *he* has been used to refer to an indefinite pronoun representing a group of men and women. This traditional pronoun use is now being questioned.

Function: agreement in number with singular antecedent *everyone*

INCORRECT

```
      s                    v    pro
```
Each one of you girls must write *your* own essay.

> **Form Used:** *your* — second person, gender?

> **Function Indicated:** agreement with antecedent *each one*, third person, feminine gender (girls)

CORRECT

```
      s                    v    pro
```
Each one of you girls must write *her* own essay.

> **Form:** *her* — third person, feminine gender

> **Function:** agreement with antecedent *each one*, third person, feminine gender

INCORRECT

```
  s      v        pro
```
One must study if *you* want to succeed.

> **Form Used:** *you* — second person

> **Function Indicated:** agreement with antecedent *one* — third person

CORRECT

```
  s      v        pro
```
One must study if *he* wants to succeed.

or

```
  s      v        pro
```
One must study if *she* wants to succeed.

> **Form:** *he* or *she* — third person singular

> **Function:** agreement with antecedent *one* — third person

Proofreading for (C) and (D) Errors
Lack of Agreement-Subject and Verb (agr)
Lack of Agreement-Pronoun and Antecedent (agr)

With the aid of the chart below, identify the errors in the sentences that follow. Any sentence that is incorrect contains no more than one error. Write both the letter and the number for all answers except (D) and (F).

(C) — lack of agreement subject and verb   C4 — verb with an indefinite pronoun
C1 — verb after a prepositional phrase   C5 — verb with a collective noun
C2 — verb in a dependent clause   D — lack of agreement pronoun and antecedent
C3 — verb after an expletive   F — correct sentence

1. The panel have reached a unanimous decision.   ____

2. Thomas, like his brothers, were often in debt.   ____

3. The more one works, the more you earn.   ____

4. Ellen is one of the students who has achieved national recognition.   ____

5. Ellen is the only one of the students who have achieved national recognition.   ____

6. There seems to be many books missing from the library.   ____

7. Each girl should bring their own notebook.   ____

8. The committee is disagreeing about the use of those funds.   ____

9. Everyone should take their turn at rowing.   ____

10. Mr. Rainville is one of those photographers who specialize in children's portraits.   ____

BONUS: Person

Write a paragraph focusing on *person:* the first person *I;* the second person *you;* or the third person *he* or *she.* Stay consistently with that person; do not shift unnecessarily from one person to another.

For example: The topic is 'Advice for a New Student.'

The person chosen is the third person: student, he or she

The task is to discuss the student (he or she) and to avoid unnecessarily shifting person by addressing the person, for example, as *you.*

Incorrect
A new student (third person) should listen to the following advice. You (second person) should be aware of school rules and regulations.

REVIEW

Proofreading for (A) — (D) Errors

With the aid of the chart below, identify the errors in the sentences that follow. Any sentence that is incorrect contains no more than one error. Write both the letter and the number for all answers except (D) and (F).

(A) — lack of parallelism
A1 — infinitive-gerund
A2 — phrase-clause
A3 — misplaced correlative
A4 — unnecessary shift in person and voice
A5 — improper series
(B) — improper case
B1 — before a gerund
B2 — predicate pronoun after linking verb
B3 — subject of an infinitive
B4 — predicate pronoun after an infinitive

B5 — direct object after a verb or verbal
B6 — object of a preposition
(C) — lack of agreement subject and verb
C1 — verb after a prepositional phrase
C2 — verb in a dependent clause
C3 — verb after an expletive
C4 — verb with an indefinite pronoun
C5 — verb with a collective noun
(D) — lack of agreement pronoun
    and antecedent
F — correct sentence

1. Grandmother approves of us spending time at our ranch in Texas. _____

2. When we visited Canada, we enjoyed not only traveling to Ottawa but also to Montreal. _____

3. The population of states such as New York and California are dense. _____

4. The testing commission attempted to create an objective test and then setting high standards. _____

5. The state writing commission is trying to determine the extent of writing difficulties within the state. _____

6. Everyone in the play knew their lines before the scheduled opening night. _____

7. The equestrian is she, the woman leading her horse toward the judging platform. _____

8. Arthur always believed his missing cousin to be him, the host of a television game show. _____

9. The news broadcast is sensational, interesting, and it is also thought-provoking. _____

10. Does he know she to be the astronaut? _____

INTRODUCTORY FORMS

Principle: The function of any introductory verbal phrase or elliptical clause is to refer logically to the subject of the sentence. (An introductory form is one that precedes the subject and the verb.)

Problem: An introductory verbal phrase or an elliptical clause that does not refer logically to the subject of the sentence is called a dangling element. The element dangles or hangs because it has no word to modify.
(Any verbal phrase placed elsewhere in the sentence may be said to dangle if it has no word to modify.)

E1. PARTICIPIAL PHRASE

INCORRECT

Daydreaming in the classroom, the clock met my gaze.

        Dangling Form: *Daydreaming in the classroom* — introductory participial phrase

        Illogical Function: adjective referring illogically to the subject *clock*

        Note: A clock cannot daydream.

CORRECT

Daydreaming in the classroom, I saw the clock.

        Introductory Form: italicized participial phrase

        Logical Function: adjective referring to the subject *I*, which has been added

E2. INFINITIVE PHRASE

INCORRECT

To play the piano well, many hours must be spent in practice.

        Dangling Form: *To play the piano well* — introductory infinitive phrase

        Illogical Function: modifier referring illogically to the subject *hours*

        Note: *Hours* cannot learn to play the piano.

CORRECT

To play the piano well, a person must practice many hours.

        Introductory Form: italicized infinitive phrase

        Logical Function: modifier referring to the subject a *person*

E3. GERUND PHRASE (Introductory Phrase Containing A Gerund)

INCORRECT

On entering the auditorium, the stage met my gaze.

        Dangling Form: *On entering the auditorium* — introductory gerund phrase

        Illogical Function: modifier referring illogically to the subject *stage*

        Note: A stage cannot walk into the auditorium.

CORRECT

On entering the auditorium, I saw the stage.

        Introductory Form: italicized gerund phrase

        Logical Function: modifier referring to the subject *I*

E4. ELLIPTICAL CLAUSE

Rule: An elliptical clause is a dependent clause with an implied subject and verb. The implied subject is assumed to be the same as the subject of the sentence.

INCORRECT

When seven years old, my $\overset{\text{S}}{\text{parents}}$ $\overset{\text{V}}{\text{bought}}$ me a bicycle.

> **Dangling Form:** *When seven years old* — introductory elliptical clause

> **Illogical Function:** element referring to the subject *parents*

> Note: The implied clause is as follows: "*When my parents were seven years old,* they bought me a bicycle."

CORRECT

When seven years old, $\overset{\text{S}}{\text{I}}$ $\overset{\text{V}}{\text{received}}$ a bicycle from my parents.

> **Introductory Form:** italicized elliptical clause

> **Logical Function:** element referring to the subject *I*

Proofreading for (E) Errors
Dangling Element (dang)

With the aid of the chart below, identify the errors in the sentences that follow. Any sentence that is incorrect contains no more than one error. Write both the letter and the number for all answers except (F).

E1 — participial phrase   E3 — gerund phrase
E2 — infinitive phrase   E4 — elliptical clause
F — correct sentence

1. Taking our seats, the game started.   _____

2. Eating potato chips and watching television, we passed the evening pleasantly.   _____

3. On entering the art gallery, the Winslow painting caught my attention.   _____

4. To write well, good books must be read.   _____

5. To catch the seven o'clock train, an early start must be made.   _____

6. When only three years old, his parents brought him to New Orleans.   _____

7. Walking across the campus, her new car met my gaze.   _____

8. After preparing the meal, the dishes were washed by me.   _____

9. Although not fully recovered from my illness, Mother insisted I begin making up my school work.   _____

10. Taken seriously ill after the first week, Anya's appointment as assistant manager was soon terminated.   _____

F. CORRECT SENTENCE

Principle
The correct sentence illustrates the proper relationship of sentence function and form.

G. DOUBLE NEGATIVE   **Proofreading Symbol: dn**

DOUBLE NEGATIVE

Principle: Two negative words should function together in a sentence only to express an affirmative statement. As in mathematics, two minuses cancel to create a positive. (In English, this use of the double negative is rare — and often confusing.)

Problem: Two negative words function together in a sentence to express a negative statement. Common negative words are as follows: *no, not, but, never, scarcely, hardly*

INCORRECT

At the rally we could *not scarcely* hear the speech of our coach.

> **Negative Forms:** *not*
> *scarcely*

CORRECT

At the rally we could scarcely hear the speech of our coach. (or — We could not hear the speech of our coach.)

INCORRECT

There can*not* be any doubt *but what* our team will win.

> **Negative Forms:** *not*
> *but what*

CORRECT

There cannot be any doubt that our team will win.

INCORRECT

I can*not* help *but* think that English is an easy subject.

> **Negative Forms:** *not*
> *but*

CORRECT

ger
I cannot help *thinking* that English is an easy subject.

> Note: A *gerund* follows the expression *cannot help.*

INCORRECT

With*out hardly* a sound, the owl swooped down on the unsuspecting mouse.

> **Negative Forms:** *out*
> *hardly*

CORRECT

With hardly a sound, the owl swooped down on the unsuspecting mouse.

Proofreading for (E) and (G) Errors
Dangling Element (dang)
Double Negative (dn)

With the aid of the chart below, identify the errors in the sentences that follow. Any sentence that is incorrect contains no more than one error. Write both the letter and the number for all answers except (G) and (F).

(E) — dangling element
E1 — participial phrase
E2 — infinitive phrase

E3 — gerund phrase
E4 — elliptical clause
G — double negative

F — correct sentence

1. Hoping to recover soon, many weeks were spent by me in the hospital. _____

2. When only an eighth grader, his father took him to Disneyland. _____

3. Sailing across the harbor, the lighthouse appeared out of the fog. _____

4. I don't hardly know what advice to give you. _____

5. To profit from experience, awareness of your successes is necessary. _____

6. My friends can't help but believe that school will last forever. _____

7. Without hardly a sound, the child toddled into the busy street. _____

8. To conquer fear, understand its cause. _____

9. After accepting the award, Jeremy scurried to his seat. _____

10. I don't hardly think that we should plan a vacation in Greece. _____

H. INCORRECT TENSE (Sequence), MOOD

Proofreading Symbol: t (tense); v (verb)

VERB TENSE AND MOOD

Principle: Verbs change form as they function to show correct tense (time) and mood (manner) of an action or a state of being.

Problem: The wrong verb form is used to show the tense or mood indicated.

H1 — H5   TENSE (TIME)

CHART OF VERB TENSES

Simple Tenses	Function	Form
Present Tense	Shows action or being happening now	I *walk*. I *am*.
Past Tense	Shows action or being completed in the past	I *walked*. I *was*.
Future Tense	Shows action or being happening at some time in the future.	I *shall* walk. I *shall* be. **Formula:** Future Tense = *will* or *shall* + the infinitive*

Perfect Tenses	Function	Form
Present Perfect Tense	Shows action or being beginning in the past and possibly continuing into the present	I *have* walked. I *have* been. **Formula:** Present Perfect Tense = *have* or *has* + the past participle*
Past Perfect Tense	Shows action or being completed before some other past action	I *had* walked. I *had* been. **Formula:** Past Perfect Tense = *had* + the past participle*
Future Perfect Tense	Shows action or being which will be completed at some future time	I *shall have* walked. I *shall have* been. **Formula:** Future Perfect Tense = *shall have* or *will have* + past participle*

* See *Appendix B* for information on principal parts of verbs.

116

H1. PRESENT PERFECT — SHOULD BE PAST

Rule: Use the past tense (form) to show action completed (function).

INCORRECT

Your friends *have called* you many times *last week*.

(S over "friends", V over "have called")

> **Form Used:** *have called* — present perfect tense

> **Function Indicated:** to show action completed —
> Clue: *last week*

CORRECT

Your friends *called* you many times *last week*.

(S over "friends", V over "called")

> **Form:** *called* — past tense

> **Function:** shows action completed

H2. PAST — SHOULD BE PRESENT PERFECT

Rule: Use the present perfect tense (form) to show action beginning in the past and extending into the present.

INCORRECT

Did you *finish* your homework *yet*?

(V over "Did", S over "you", V over "finish")

> **Form Used:** *did finish* — past tense

> **Function Indicated:** to show action beginning in the past and extending into the present —
> Clue: *yet* (The assignment may not be completed.)

CORRECT

v   s   v

Have you *finished* your homework *yet?*

> **Form:** *have finished* — present perfect tense
>
> **Function:** shows action beginning in the past and extending into the present

H3. PAST — SHOULD BE PAST PERFECT

> **Rule:** Use the past perfect tense to show past action completed before some other past action.

INCORRECT

s   v

Yesterday I *found* my tennis racquet where I *left* it in Father's car last week.

> **Form Used:** *left* — past tense
>
> **Function Indicated:** to show past action completed before some other past action

Two actions occurred in the *past.*
   The finding: yesterday
   The leaving: last week
The *leaving* occurred before the *finding.*
Therefore, the past perfect tense is needed.

CORRECT

s   v

Yesterday I *found* my tennis racquet where I *had left* it in Father's car last week.

> **Form:** *had left* — past perfect tense
>
> **Function:** shows action completed before some other past action

H4. PERFECT INFINITIVE — SHOULD BE PRESENT INFINITIVE

> **Rule:** Use the present infinitive to show action *contemporaneous with/or future to* that of the main verb. Use the perfect infinitive to show action *prior to* that of the main verb.

INCORRECT

<pre>
  S   V
He would have liked <i>to have visited</i> the museum last month.
</pre>

Form Used: *to have visited* — perfect infinitive
would have liked — main verb

Function Indicated: to show present action — the *desiring* occurred before (prior to) the *visiting* (or not visiting)

CORRECT

<pre>
  S   V
He would have liked <i>to visit</i> the museum last month.
</pre>

Form: *to visit* — present infinitive

Function: shows action future to that of main verb, *would have liked*

H5. SEQUENCE (Following)

Note: Whenever two or more verbs exist in a single sentence, sequence occurs. Usually, the main verb of the sentence is the *constant* verb. The verb(s) in the dependent clause or the verbals are the variables. They change form to follow the time established by the main verb. The examples under *H5* simply stress two particular instances of sequencing.

Rule 1: When the verb in an indirect quotation follows a main verb which is in the past tense, use the following helping verbs: *should, would, could, might.* When the verb in an indirect quotation follows a main verb which is in the present or future tense, use the following helping verbs: *shall, will, can, may.*

INCORRECT

<pre>
              S   V
Our class advisor <i>said</i> last week that she <i>may permit</i> us to hold a fund-raising dance.
</pre>

Form Used: *may permit* — present tense

Function Indicated: to show past action following the main verb, *said*, past tense

CORRECT

$\overset{\text{s}}{\text{Our class advisor}} \overset{\text{v}}{said}$ last week that she *might permit* us to hold a fund-raising dance.

      Form: *might permit* — past tense

      Function: shows past action — following the main verb, *said*, past tense

Rule 2: Use the present tense to show a 'timeless truth' expressed in a noun clause.

INCORRECT

$\overset{\text{s}}{\text{Franklin}} \overset{\text{v}}{\text{proved}}$ that lightning *was* electricity.

      Form Used: *was* — past tense

      Function Indicated: to show action indicating a timeless truth — lightning is still electricity.

CORRECT

$\overset{\text{s}}{\text{Franklin}} \overset{\text{v}}{\text{proved}}$ that lightning *is* electricity.

      Form: *is* — present tense

      Function: shows timeless truth

H6. SUBJUNCTIVE MOOD

Rule: Verbs change form as they function to show changes in mood (manner).

<hr>

CHART OF MOOD

Mood	Function	Form
Indicative	Shows a fact or asks a question	He *works*. Does he work?
Imperative	Shows a command or request	*Work* now. Please work today.
Subjunctive	Shows a contrary-to-fact condition	He wishes he *were* at home. (He is not)
	In the subjunctive mood, the first and third person singular take plural verb forms. This rule most commonly affects forms of the verb *to be*.	If he *were* at home, he would be happy. (He is not at home).
	Use *were* instead of *was* (in the first and third person singular) to show a wish or contrary-to-fact condition in a dependent clause.	

<hr>

INCORRECT

                    s   v

If I *was* in Venice now, I would be happy.

       Form Used: *was* — indicative mood

       Function Indicated: to show a contrary-to-fact condition

       Note: I am not in Venice.

CORRECT

                    s   v

If I *were* in Venice now, I would be happy.

       Form: *were* — subjunctive mood

       Function: shows contrary-to-fact condition

Proofreading for (H) Errors

Incorrect Tense (Sequence), Mood (t, v)

With the aid of the chart below, identify the errors in the sentences that follow. Any sentence that is incorrect contains no more than one error. Write both the letter and the number for all answers except (F).

H1 — present perfect for past   H4 — perfect infinitive for present
H2 — past for present perfect   H5 — sequence
H3 — past for past perfect   H6 — subjunctive mood
F — correct sentence

(#1)

1. The guidance director said that we can elect six courses. _____

2. Did you finish the *Iliad* yet? _____

3. If I were in Ireland, I would be happy. _____

4. I should have liked to have visited you last week. _____

5. She wishes she was at the beach. _____

6. She has warned you several times last evening. _____

7. The student entered military service after she graduated from high school. _____

8. Why has he just called you? _____

9. If she was riding her motorcycle now, she would feel free. _____

10. I should have liked to live in Washington's time. _____

Proofreading for (H) Errors

(#2)

1. Franklin proved that lightning is electricity. _____

2. Suddenly he remembered that he promised to meet her at eight. _____

3. The children were disappointed because they had hoped to have gone with us. _____

4. The principal said that we can have a dance in May. _____

5. If he was taller, he would be a champion. _____

6. Did you plant the tomatoes yet? _____

7. Mother says that we may attend the square-dance. _____

8. I wish I was home now. _____

9. Have you finished the project last evening? _____

10. I should have liked to have visited you on Sunday. _____

BONUS: Tense

Beware: The Sophisticated Shift

Write a composition in a predetermined tense such as the *present tense* or the *past tense*. Make a conscious effort to use that tense consistently, especially in sentences and main clauses. Many students who avoid most of the "common errors" make the sophisticated shift — an unnecessary shift in tense.

Note: Checking for unnecessary shifts in tense is especially important in the final proofreading of any composition.

Proofreading for (G) and (H) Errors
Double Negative (dn)
Incorrect Tense (Sequence), Mood (t, v)

With the aid of the chart below, identify the errors in the sentences that follow. Any sentence that is incorrect contains no more than one error. Write both the letter and the number for all answers except (G) and (F).

G — double negative
(H) — incorrect tense, sequence, mood
H1 — present perfect for past
H2 — past for present perfect

H3 — past for past perfect
H4 — perfect infinitive for present
H5 — sequence
H6 — subjunctive mood

F — correct sentence

1. Did you finish that science report already? ____

2. If he was in Arizona, he would visit the Painted Desert. ____

3. Terry said that she would like to have lived in Leonardo da Vinci's time. ____

4. When Theodora visited the Louvre in Paris, she viewed the "Mona Lisa" after she admired the well known Greek sculpture, the "Venus de Milo." ____

5. The sentry said that we cannot enter the armory. ____

6. After he saw the movie *The African Queen*, Kirk watched another Bogart classic *Casablanca*. ____

7. Norma has finished her chores an hour ago. ____

8. The sergeant said that the two privates can have a weekend pass. ____

9. I don't hardly know how to finish this calculus assignment. ____

10. I wish I were in Honolulu now. ____

REVIEW
Proofreading for (A) — (H) Errors (#1)

With the aid of the chart below, identify the errors in the sentences that follow. Any sentence that is incorrect contains no more than one error. Write both the letter and the number for all answers except (D), (F), and (G).

(A) — lack of parallelism
A1 — infinitive — gerund
A2 — phrase — clause
A3 — misplaced correlatives
A4 — unnecessary shift in person and voice
A5 — improper series
(B) — improper case
B1 — before a gerund
B2 — predicate pronoun after a linking verb
B3 — subject of an infinitive
B4 — predicate noun after an infinitive
B5 — direct object after a verb or verbal
B6 — object of a preposition
(C) — lack of agreement subject-verb
C1 — verb after a prepositional phrase
C2 — verb in a dependent clause
C3 — verb after an expletive

C4 — verb with an indefinite pronoun
C5 — verb with a collective noun
D — lack of agreement pronoun-antecedent
(E) — dangling element
E1 — participial phrase
E2 — infinitive phrase
E3 — gerund phrase
E4 — elliptical clause
F — correct sentence
G — double negative
(H) — incorrect tense, sequence, mood
H1 — present perfect for past
H2 — past for present perfect
H3 — past for past perfect
H4 — perfect infinitive for present
H5 — sequence
H6 — subjunctive mood

1. When six years old, his grandparents sent him to boarding school. _____

2. Uncle Thad told us that Father knew she to be the missing heiress. _____

3. If I was a jet pilot, I would be happy. _____

4. The master of ceremonies was intelligent, congenial, and he was also courteous. _____

5. Nobody in the audience knows what the speakers will say about foreign affairs. _____

6. Last night I studied for some time and then my car was washed by me. _____

7. Filing letters in the office, the missing memo was found. _____

8. I should have like to have seen you last week. _____

9. He entered Smith Academy after he returned from Hawaii. _____

10. She will win the election because of her composure and because she speaks confidently. _____

11. I can't help but think this assignment is difficult. _____

125

12. Tom Smith is one of those students who has been inducted into the National Honor Society. _____

13. The traffic officer has warned you several times yesterday. _____

14. All but Bill and he own cars. _____

15. Driving on the freeway, the billboard could be seen for miles. _____

16. The meteorologist says that we could expect rain. _____

17. Ann disapproves of Paul joining the Peace Corps. _____

18. Did you read the government report yet? _____

19. There seems to be hundreds of birds in that aviary. _____

20. The council agrees on the issue. _____

REVIEW
Proofreading for (A) — (H) Errors (#2)

With the aid of the chart below, identify the errors in the sentences that follow. Any sentence that is incorrect contains no more than one error. Write both the letter and the number for all answers except (D), (F), and (G).

(A) — lack of parallelism
A1 — infinitive — gerund
A2 — phrase — clause
A3 — misplaced correlatives
A4 — unnecessary shift in person and voice
A5 — improper series
(B) — improper case
B1 — before a gerund
B2 — predicate pronoun after a linking verb
B3 — subject of an infinitive
B4 — predicate noun after an infinitive
B5 — direct object after a verb or verbal
(C) — lack of agreement subject-verb
C1 — verb after a prepositional phrase
C2 — verb in a dependent clause
C3 — verb after an expletive

C4 — verb with an indefinite pronoun
C5 — verb with a collective noun
D — lack of agreement pronoun-antecedent
(E) — dangling element
E1 — participial phrase
E2 — infinitive phrase
E3 — gerund phrase
E4 — elliptical clause
F — correct sentence
G — double negative
(H) — incorrect tense, sequence, mood
H1 — present perfect for past
H2 — past for present perfect
H3 — past for past perfect
H4 — perfect infinitive for present
H5 — sequence
H6 — subjunctive mood

1. The new student was handsome, reliable, and he was also congenial. _____

2. Ms. Cole is her, the person holding the camera. _____

3. She became an auto mechanic after she completed high school. _____

4. Walking in the park, the garden met my gaze. _____

5. I should have liked to have seen you two hours ago. _____

6. When five years old, her parents gave her a bicycle. _____

7. Everyone entered the vocational school except Jim and I. _____

8. She likes to plant the tomatoes and weeding the garden. _____

9. During the vacation I went to Boston, and then shopping was done by me. _____

10. Nola resigned her position because of her illness and because she was bored. _____

11. Has he seen the latest movies last night? _____

127

12. The jury is disagreeing on the issue. ____

13. They cannot help believing that optimism is more beneficial than pessimism. ____

14. Matthew is efficient not only at school but also at the office. ____

15. The meteorologist said this morning that we cannot hope for a sunny day. ____

16. We disapprove of you leaving early. ____

17. Tony is one of those students who has been sent to the office. ____

18. Running on the sidewalk, the elm tree met my gaze. ____

19. Everyone in the class is doing their art project. ____

20. Who are you planning to invite to the rally? ____

With the aid of the chart below, identify the errors in the sentences that follow. Any sentence that is incorrect contains no more than one error. Write both the letter and the number for all answers except (D), (F), and (G).

(A) — lack of parallelism	C4 — verb with an indefinite pronoun
A1 — infinitive — gerund	C5 — verb with a collective noun
A2 — phrase — clause	D — lack of agreement pronoun-antecedent
A3 — misplaced correlatives	(E) — dangling element
A4 — unnecessary shift in person and voice	E1 — participial phrase
A5 — improper series	E2 — infinitive phrase
(B) — improper case	E3 — gerund phrase
B1 — before a gerund	E4 — elliptical clause
B2 — predicate pronoun after a linking verb	F — correct sentence
	G — double negative
B3 — subject of an infinitive	(H) — incorrect tense, sequence, mood
B4 — predicate noun after an infinitive	H1 — present perfect for past
B5 — direct object after a verb or verbal	H2 — past for present perfect
B6 — object of a preposition	H3 — past for past perfect
(C) — lack of agreement subject-verb	H4 — perfect infinitive for present
C1 — verb after a prepositional phrase	H5 — sequence
C2 — verb in a dependent clause	H6 — subjunctive mood
C3 — verb after an expletive	

1. Her favorite hobbies are reading and to watch television. ⸺

2. Our teacher is fair not only in his grading but also in his testing. ⸺

3. When five years old, his parents took him to a jazz festival. ⸺

4. The reporter said yesterday that we cannot hope for regional conferences. ⸺

5. I know she to be an auto safety consultant. ⸺

6. I approve of her leaving the government post because she cannot support the Commerce Department's new auto safety standards. ⸺

7. If I was in Florida, I should visit Cape Canaveral. ⸺

8. The attorney is one of those authors who has written a controversial book. ⸺

9. Her book review was appropriate, instructive, and it was also accurate. ⸺

10. Strolling down the street, the police station met my gaze. ⸺

11. There can be no doubt but that the volcano will erupt. ⸺

12. Everyone taking this test is checking their answers carefully. ____

13. Yesterday he talked in study hall and then a detention slip was issued to him. ____

14. Who are you selecting as queen of the Junior Prom? ____

15. On reading the bestseller, the controversial issue became known. ____

16. I should have liked to have toured Europe last summer. ____

17. To concentrate effectively, the room must be quiet. ____

18. The weather bureau has warned us several times yesterday about the approaching hurricane. ____

19. We called the child's mother, after we treated his injured hand. ____

20. All will participate in the fashion show but Sally and he. ____

I. INCOMPLETE SENTENCE (Fragment)

SENTENCE

Principle: A sentence is a group of words that expresses a complete thought.
It contains a verb, its subject, and any related complements and modifiers. It begins with a capital letter and ends with a punctuation mark.

Problem: A sentence fragment is a group of words that does not express a complete thought. It frequently occurs because a sentence form, such as a phrase or a clause, is written as if it were a sentence. (The writer intends the sentence form to be part of a sentence, but isolates this form from the sentence by faulty punctuation and thus creates a sentence fragment.)

Remember: *Always check sentence completeness by reading from the capital letter to the end mark and by asking whether the word group makes sense alone.*

II. DEPENDENT CLAUSE

INCORRECT

                                                      s   v
After they had completed the race. The runners rested in the shade.

> **Isolated Form:** *after they had completed the race* — dependent clause punctuated as if it were a sentence

> **Intended Function:** adverb modifying the verb *rested* in the sentence following

CORRECT

                                                      s   v
After they had completed the race, the runners rested in the shade.

> **Included Form:** italicized introductory clause

> **Correct Function:** adverb modifying the main verb *rested*

12. INFINITIVE PHRASE

INCORRECT

To compete in the contest. We had to register by June 1.

Isolated Form: *To compete in the contest* — infinitive phrase punctuated as if it were a sentence (Note the period after *contest.*)

Intended Function: modifier referring to the subject *we* in the sentence following

CORRECT

To compete in the contest, we had to register by June 1.

Included Form: italicized introductory infinitive phrase

Correct Function: modifier of subject *we*

13. PARTICIPIAL PHRASE

INCORRECT

Entering the office building. Janet was stopped by a security guard.

Isolated Form: *entering the office building* — participial phrase punctuated as if it were a sentence

Intended Function: adjective modifying the subject *Janet* in the sentence following

CORRECT

Entering the office building, Janet was stopped by a security guard.

Included Form: italicized introductory participial phrase

Correct Function: adjective modifying the subject *Janet*

I4. APPOSITIVE

INCORRECT

    s   v

She enjoys all of her courses. *English, algebra, social science, and French.*

> **Isolated Form:** *English, algebra, social science, and French* — appositive punctuated as if it were a sentence

> **Intended Function:** appositive renaming the word *courses* in the preceding sentence

CORRECT

    s   v

She enjoys all her courses, *English, algebra, social science, and French.*

> **Included Form:** italicized appositive

> **Correct Function:** appositive renaming the word *courses*

Proofreading for (I) Errors
Fragment (frag)

With the aid of the chart below, identify the errors in the sentences that follow. Any sentence that is incorrect contains no more than one error. Write both the letter and the number for all answers except (F).

I1 — dependent clause   I3 — participial phrase
I2 — infinitive phrase   I4 — appositive
                   F — correct sentence

1. Yesterday I left school early. Because I was ill. _____

2. To speak Spanish fluently. One should travel in Spain. _____

3. The author, preparing to work, gathered her materials. A typewriter, an eraser, and heavy-weight paper. _____

4. Singing in the school chorus. Liane improved her voice. _____

5. When he entered the room, he saw the toys: dolls, trucks, and games. _____

6. Entering her office, the principal saw the student. A freshman who had lost all of her books. _____

7. To enjoy that novel, a person should study its historical background first. _____

8. Now I know that winter is approaching. The squirrels are gathering acorns. _____

9. If the contractors have completed work on the highway on time. They will have met the terms of the contract. _____

10. Trying to finish his composition. Jack became discouraged. _____

PRONOUN REFERENCE

Principle: A pronoun stands for a noun, or another pronoun, called its *antecedent*.

Problem: The pronoun has no stated antecedent; the pronoun refers confusingly to two different antecedents.

J1. VAGUE

Rule: Vague reference occurs when the pronoun has no definite antecedent. Be sure that a word such as *this, which, it* has a specific antecedent. Such a pronoun must refer to a specific noun or pronoun. It cannot refer to an entire clause.

INCORRECT

s   v
Mike is usually courteous which pleases his teachers.

> **Form Used:** *which* — pronoun

> **Function Indicated:** vague — There is no antecedent in the sentence. *Which* refers to what?

CORRECT

s   v
Mike's usual courtesy is a habit which pleases his teachers.

> **Form:** *which* — pronoun

> **Function:** refers to antecedent *habit*

J2. AMBIGUOUS

Rule: Ambiguous reference occurs when a pronoun refers to two different antecedents.

INCORRECT

s   v
Elaine's aunt told her that *she* needs a vacation.

Form Used: *she* — pronoun

Function Indicated: ambiguous — Does *she* refer to Elaine or to Elaine's aunt? Who needs the vacation?

CORRECT

      s   v
Elaine's aunt told her, "I need a vacation."

or

      s   v
Elaine's aunt told her, "You need a vacation."

Now the ambiguity has been eliminated.

Proofreading for (I) and (J) Errors
Fragment (frag)
Reference (ref)

With the aid of the chart below, identify the errors in the sentences that follow. Any sentence that is incorrect contains no more than one error. Write both the letter and the number for all answers except (F).

(I) — fragment
I1 — dependent clause
I2 — infinitive phrase
I3 — participial phrase

I4 — appositive
(J) — reference
J1 — vague reference
J2 — ambiguous reference

F — correct sentence

(#1)

1. Henry lives in Avon. A friendly town in Massachusetts. ——

2. They sell insurance in Hartford. ——

3. Mary told Jill that she had received an 'A.' ——

4. To think clearly. A person must eliminate confusing ideas. ——

5. She is truthful which is commendable. ——

6. Requesting permission to leave. The child waved her hand constantly. ——

7. I found the book. Have you read it? ——

8. When we return from hunting. Let's have a cup of hot chocolate. ——

9. She really enjoys polo, a game played by two teams of players on horseback. ——

10. The view from our house is beautiful which pleases us. ——

11. We traveled in Canada. They are hospitable people. ——

Proofreading for (I) and (J) Errors

(#2)

1. He finally completed computer training which pleased him. ——

2. To reach the airport on time. Leave home by five o'clock. ——

3. Brenda told Joanne that she needs a new radio.   ——

4. Watching from the tower. Alexa spotted the lost child.   ——

5. A prolific writer. She wrote short stories, novels, plays, and poems.   ——

6. Elizabeth was often absent which annoyed her teachers.   ——

7. Riding in the super jet. Ted forgot his troubles.   ——

8. He enjoys reading the stories of O'Henry. A writer famous for his surprise endings.   ——

9. If you receive a phone call, notify me immediately.   ——

10. One of the students told the teacher that she was an expert in mathematics.   ——

K. FAULTY PUNCTUATION OF RESTRICTIVE AND NONRESTRICTIVE SENTENCE ELEMENTS

Proofreading Symbol: p

PUNCTUATION OF RESTRICTIVE-NONRESTRICTIVE ELEMENTS

Principle: *Restrictive* sentence elements are sentence elements essential to a sentence; they should not be set off by commas.
Nonrestrictive sentence elements are not necessary to the sentence meaning. They should be set off by commas.

Problem: Restrictive forms are set off by commas; nonrestrictive forms are not set off by commas.

K1. ADJECTIVE CLAUSE

INCORRECT

Her brother *who is a senior in college* drove her to school this morning.

> **Form:** *who is a senior in college* — dependent clause

> **Function:** adjective adding extra information only — Commas are necessary to set off the nonrestrictive information.

CORRECT

Her brother, *who is a senior in college*, drove her to school this morning.

> **Form:** italicized adjective clause set off by commas

> **Function:** adjective adding nonrestrictive information

INCORRECT

All students, *who are going on the field trip*, should report to the office.

> **Form:** *who are going on the field trip* — dependent clause

> **Function:** adjective giving essential information — Commas should be omitted. The restrictive information is necessary. Note: All students in the school should not report to the office, only those going on the field trip.

CORRECT

$\overset{\text{s}}{\text{All students}}$ *who are going on the field trip* $\overset{\text{v}}{\text{should report}}$ to the office.

> **Form:** italicized adjective clause
>
> **Function:** adjective telling "*which* students?" should report — Commas have been omitted. The restrictive information is essential.

INCORRECT

$\overset{\text{s}}{\text{Hockey}}$ $\overset{\text{v}}{\text{is}}$ the game, *that I like best.*

> **Form:** *that I like best* — adjective clause
>
> **Function:** adjective stating essential information, telling "*which* game?" — Commas should be omitted.

CORRECT

$\overset{\text{s}}{\text{Hockey}}$ $\overset{\text{v}}{\text{is}}$ the game *that I like best.*

> **Form:** italicized adjective clause
>
> **Function:** adjective giving restrictive information — Comma has been omitted. Note: A clause beginning with *that* is usually essential. It should not be set off from the sentence.

K2. PARTICIPIAL PHRASE

INCORRECT

$\overset{\text{s}}{\text{His cousin}}$ *working in the main office* $\overset{\text{v}}{\text{heard}}$ the news first.

> **Form:** *working in the main office* — participial phrase
>
> **Function:** adjective giving additional (nonessential) information about his cousin. Commas are needed.

CORRECT

$\overset{\text{s}}{\text{His cousin}}$, *working in the main office,* $\overset{\text{v}}{\text{heard}}$ the news first.

140

Form: italicized participial phrase

Function: adjective adding nonessential information — The nonrestrictive element has been set off by commas.

INCORRECT

s   v

His cousin is the girl, *now working in the main office.*

    Form: *now working in the main office* — participial phrase

    Function: adjective adding essential information, telling *"which* girl?" — Comma should be omitted.

CORRECT

s   v

His cousin is the girl *now working in the main office.*

    Form: italicized participial phrase

    Function: adjective giving essential information — The comma has been omitted.

    Note: Who decides ultimately whether information is essential or nonessential? The writer decides.

K3. APPOSITIVE

INCORRECT

s   v

A Doll's House a play by Ibsen deals with current problems.

    Form: *a play by Ibsen* — appositive

    Function: appositive giving additional information only — Commas are needed for nonrestrictive information.

CORRECT

s   v

A Doll's House, a play by Ibsen, deals with current problems.

Form: italicized appositive

Function: appositive giving additional information renaming *A Doll's House*. Nonrestrictive element is set off by commas.

INCORRECT

  s   v
Ibsen's play, *A Doll's House*, deals with current problems.

> **Form:** *A Doll's House* — appositive

> **Function:** appositive giving necessary information — Commas should be omitted.

CORRECT

  s   v
Ibsen's play *A Doll's House* deals with current problems.

> **Form:** italicized appositive

> **Function:** appositive stating restrictive information

Proofreading for (K) Errors
Faulty Punctuation of Restrictive
Or Nonrestrictive Elements (p)

With the aid of the chart below, identify the errors in the sentences that follow. Any sentence that is incorrect contains no more than one error. Write both the letter and the number for all answers except (F).

K1 — adjective clause   K3 — appositive
K2 — participial phrase   F — correct sentence

1. Virginia Wolfe's novel, *Mrs. Dalloway,* is seldom studied in high school.   ——

2. Everyone, who wishes to pass this test, should attend the help session.   ——

3. When you visit Mystic Seaport, a replica of a 19th century fishing village, you will see interesting nautical relics.   ——

4. Did you know that London's Saint Paul's Cathedral located at the head of Ludgate Hill was designed by Sir Christopher Wren?   ——

5. Her brother Ted, looking out the window, noticed the injured animal first.   ——

6. The city that she loves is San Francisco.   ——

7. Baker, a biographer of Hemingway, taught at Middlebury College.   ——

8. Mrs. Malaprop is a famous character in Sheridan's play, *The Rivals.*   ——

9. Any athlete, who participated in the Olympics, should be honored.   ——

10. Her cousin Louis who is an enthusiastic lacrosse player attends Temple University.   ——

CONSECUTIVE COMPLETE THOUGHTS

Principle: Consecutive complete thoughts that are closely related should be written as separate sentences or should be joined correctly as independent clauses in a compound sentence.

Problem: Consecutive complete thoughts are joined incorrectly by a comma. *A comma splices or cuts the two complete thoughts.* It creates, therefore, a *comma splice.*

L1. COMMA ALONE

INCORRECT

           S   V   S   V
Poe's stories are exciting, they are full of terrifying experiences.

> **Joined Forms:** the italicized complete thoughts — incorrectly joined in a single sentence by a comma
>
> **Intended Functions:** expressions of two complete thoughts

CORRECT

— Poe's stories are exciting.
   They are full of terrifying experiences.
   — *Now both forms function as sentences.*
— Poe's stories are exciting; they are full of terrifying experiences. (A semi-colon (;) joins the independent clauses in a compound sentence.)
— Poe's stories are exciting: they are full of terrifying experiences. (A colon (:) joins the independent clause in a compound sentence.)
   — *Now both forms function as independent clauses in a compound sentence.*
Note: Some experts prefer the colon to the semi-colon in the above example since the second clause explains the first: it tells *why*.

L2. COMMA BEFORE A CONJUNCTIVE ADVERB

Rule: Conjunctive adverbs are words such as *however, moreover, nevertheless, so, yet, thus*, and *then*. When a conjunctive adverb joins the independent clauses in a compound sentence, it is preceded by a semi-colon.

INCORRECT

s   v   s   v
Petra was absent on Friday, consequently, *she missed the chemistry test.*

> **Joined Forms:** the italicized complete thoughts — incorrectly joined in a single sentence by a comma preceding the conjunctive adverb *consequently*
>
> **Intended Functions:** expressions of two independent clauses in a single sentence

CORRECT

s   v   s   v
Petra was absent on Friday; consequently, she missed the chemistry test.

> Now both forms function as the independent clauses of a compound sentence, correctly joined with the semi-colon preceding the conjunctive adverb.

L3. COMMA WITH QUOTATION MARKS

INCORRECT

"*I plan to travel in England,*" my friend said happily, "*I want to visit Shakespeare's birthplace.*"

> **Joined Forms:** italicized complete thoughts — incorrectly joined by the comma following *happily* because of confusion with quotation marks
>
> Note: The speaker made two statements: "I plan to travel in England." "I want to visit Shakespeare's birthplace."
>
> **Intended Functions:** expressions of two sentences

CORRECT

"I plan to travel in England," my friend said happily. "I want to visit Shakespeare's birthplace."

> Now both forms function as separate sentences.

Proofreading for (L) Errors
Comma Splice (cs)

With the aid of the chart below, identify the errors in the sentences that follow. Any sentence that is incorrect contains no more than one error. Write both the letter and the number for all answers except (F).

L1 — comma alone   L3 — comma with quotation marks
L2 — comma before a conjunctive adverb   F — correct sentence

1. "Answer only the first five questions," he said, "The testing time is extremely limited." _____

2. We will leave for Japan immediately, therefore, we will complete that project in the fall. _____

3. To be a successful office worker, you should master certain skills, you should know how to file and to type. _____

4. "The next chapter is easy," said the teacher, "The main ideas are clearly marked." _____

5. Our friend from Oregon visited our family recently; however, he left early, for he wanted to travel throughout New England. _____

6. "The nine o'clock class has been canceled," said the teacher. "It has been rescheduled for a later time." _____

7. "Why are you crying?" she asked, "Are you lost?" _____

8. No one expected her to become a numismatist, she had never been interested in coins. _____

9. When you finish your homework, please read that novel, it is a science fiction story with a horrifying ending. _____

10. The children, who were playing innocently in the park, saw the accident, however, they were too frightened to relate the details of the mishap. _____

Proofreading for (K) and (L) Errors
Restrictive — Nonrestrictive Element (p)
Comma Splice (cs)

With the aid of the chart below, identify the errors in the sentences that follow. Any sentence that is incorrect contains no more than one error. Write both the letter and the number for all answers except (F).

(K) — faulty punctuation of restrictive or nonrestrictive elements	(L) — comma fault
K1 — adjective clause	L1 — comma alone
K2 — participial phrase	L2 — comma before a conjunctive adverb
K3 — appositive	L3 — comma with quotation marks
	F — correct sentence

1. George arrived in New Jersey on Tuesday, therefore, he visited his cousins in Passaic. _____

2. The plane left Boston on schedule, it arrived in New York very late because of a snow storm. _____

3. Dicken's novel, *A Tale of Two Cities*, is set in London and Paris. _____

4. All passengers, who are traveling with United Airlines, should prepare to depart. _____

5. Because my sister, Evelyn, is a bright child, my parents sent her to a local Montessori school; my sister Jean is also bright, but she refuses to attend the school. _____

6. "Please open the door," she cried, "I cannot walk a step farther tonight." _____

7. The old man, watching a television program, fell asleep in the den. _____

8. She left early; however, she arrived late. _____

9. Everyone who knew him liked him. _____

10. All students who plan to attend the track meet should buy tickets immediately. _____

147

REVIEW
Proofreading for (I) — (L) Errors

With the aid of the chart below, identify the errors in the sentences that follow. Any sentence that is incorrect contains no more than one error. Write both the letter and the number for all answers except (F).

(I) — fragment	K1 — adjective clause
I1 — dependent clause	K2 — participial phrase
I2 — infinitive phrase	K3 — appositive
I3 — participial phrase	(L) — comma splice
I4 — appositive	L1 — comma alone
(J) — faulty reference	L2 — comma before a conjunctive adverb
J1 — vague reference	
J2 — ambiguous reference	L3 — comma with quotation marks
(K) — faulty punctuation of restrictive and nonrestrictive elements	(F) — correct sentence

1. Whenever Fred presented a cogent argument. The teacher refused to listen to him. ____

2. The most erudite student was Frances; she pursued all her scholarly endeavors diligently. ____

3. Ken's teacher told him that he should see a mneumonic expert. ____

4. Your ideas are eclectic, Mona, they are not coherent. ____

5. His sister insists that she is not fickle, however, she has broken two engagements this year. ____

6. Ernest lives like a nomad, he roams from one town to the next. ____

7. To win the debate, Marlene. You must present relevant arguments. ____

8. My best friend types well; however, he refuses to teach it to me. ____

9. Her dog was extremely loyal which pleased her. ____

10. "Your giving us the money is a generous deed," said the chairperson, "The committee certainly appreciates your magnanimity." ____

11. The little girl wanted her mother to read Louisa May Alcott's novel, *Little Women*. ____

12. Henry David Thoreau, a lover of nature, wrote the famous book *Walden*. ____

13. Steve an uninterested student becomes drowsy whenever Mr. Blake discusses Austen's novel *Emma*. ____

14. "Education develops your mind," said Ms. Baker. "Please pay attention to this passage." ____

15. Phyllis always begins her compositions with a rhetorical question. A question used primarily for stylistic effect. _____

16. They teach chemistry at Brookville High School. _____

17. "My dilemma is obvious," said Philip, "I don't know whether to join the debating team." _____

18. Working in the laboratory. Janet missed the film. _____

19. When the filmstrip broke. The class clapped with glee. _____

20. Siegred joined the Forensic Society. Because she enjoyed debates. _____

M. MISPLACED MODIFIERS AND APPOSITIVES

Proofreading Symbol: mp; arr (arrangement)

PLACEMENT OF MODIFIERS AND APPOSITIVES

Principle: Word, phrase, and clause modifiers should be placed as close as possible to the words that they emphasize or modify. Appositives should be placed as close as possible to the words that they rename.

Problem: Word, phrase, and clause modifiers function incorrectly or illogically because they have been misplaced. Appositives rename illogically because they have been misplaced.

M1. WORD

Rule: An emphasizing modifier such as *only, just,* or *even* should be placed as close as possible to the word(s) emphasized.

INCORRECT

I *only* saw Shirley at the game, no one else.

> **Misplaced Form:** *only* — incorrectly placed

> **Incorrect Function:** modifier emphasizing the verb *saw*
> Clue: The expression *no one else* indicates that *Shirley* should be emphasized.

CORRECT

I saw *only* Shirley at the game, no one else.

> **Form:** *only* — word correctly placed before *Shirley*

> **Function:** modifier emphasizing *Shirley*

INCORRECT

I saw *only* Shirley at the game, not at the party.

> **Misplaced Form:** *only* — incorrectly placed near *Shirley*

> **Incorrect Function:** modifier emphasizing *Shirley*
> Clue: The expression *not at the party* indicates that the similar phrase *at the game* should be emphasized.

CORRECT

I saw Shirley *only* at the game, not at the party.

> **Form:** *only* — placed before *at the game*

> **Function:** modifier correctly emphasizing the phrase

> Note: The writer ultimately decides the point of emphasis.

M2. PHRASE

> **Rule:** A modifying phrase should be placed as close as possible to the word it modifies.

INCORRECT

We saw an advertisement for a student who can type *on the bulletin board.*

> **Misplaced Form:** *on the bulletin board* — prepositional phrase

> **Illogical Function:** adverb — modifying the verb *type*
> — answering the question "type *where?*"

> Note: The intention is not for the student to type on the bulletin board.

CORRECT

We saw *on the bulletin board* an advertisement for a student who can type.

> **Form:** *on the bulletin board* — prepositional phrase

> **Function:** adverb — modifying the verb *saw*
> — answering the question "saw *where?*"

Note: If the verb has both an adverb modifier and a complement that also has a modifier, remember to insert the modifier of the verb first. (In the correct example, the *where* is placed before the *what*.)

I saw (where?)
  on the bulletin board — adverb
(what?)
  an advertisement — direct object
(what kind of advertisement?)
  for a student who can type — adjective phrase

M3. CLAUSE

Rule: A modifying clause should be placed as close as possible to the word(s) that it modifies.

INCORRECT

My father has given my mother a new summer home in Vermont, *which he designed and built.*

  Misplaced Form: *which he designed and built* — dependent clause

  Illogical Function: adjective — modifying the word *Vermont*

  Note: He did not design and build the state.

CORRECT

My father gave my mother a new summer home *which he designed and built* in Vermont.

  Form: *which he designed and built* — dependent clause

  Function: adjective correctly placed
    — modifying the word *house*
    — answering the question "*which* house?"

M4. APPOSITIVE

INCORRECT

An ardent fan, all baseball games were attended faithfully by Jack.

      Misplaced Form: *An ardent fan* — noun phrase

      Illogical Function: appositive — renaming the subject *games*

CORRECT

An ardent fan, Jack attended all baseball games faithfully.

      Form: *An ardent fan* — noun phrase

      Function: appositive — correctly renaming the subject *Jack*

Proofreading for (M) Errors
Incorrect Position (mp)

With the aid of the chart below, identify the errors in the sentences that follow. Any sentence that is incorrect contains no more than one error. Write both the letter and the number for all answers except (F).

M1 — word   M3 — clause
M2 — phrase   M4 — appositive
                    F — correct sentence

1. We only traveled in the summer, not in the winter.   ——

2. Aunt Paula placed the vase in the room which she had purchased.   ——

3. I only saw Sally at the party, not Jack or Alice.   ——

4. An enthusiastic antique collector, every auction was attended by her cousin Sharon.   ——

5. They saw an advertisement for a person who can sell cars in the newspaper.   ——

6. He rode only the pony, not the stallion.   ——

7. A happy child, many hours were spent playing by his sister Margaret.   ——

8. He works during the evening and he even works during the spring vacation.   ——

9. Uncle Ted read that his favorite candidate had been elected in the Sunday newspaper.   ——

10. The child carried a balloon in his hand which was purple.   ——

BONUS: Placement of Modifiers

Make a poster illustrating a ridiculous (M) error.

For example: *Aunt Bluebelle said that she would arrive on Saturday in her letter.*

Give both the incorrect sentence and the correct sentence on your poster.

Make a poster illustrating three correct uses of the word *only* in similar sentences.

For example: *Dan rode only the bronco, not the burro.*

Dan only attempted to ride the bronco; he fell off.

Only Dan rode the bronco; Phil and Win just watched.

Proofreading for (K), (L), and (M) Errors

With the aid of the chart below, identify the errors in the sentences that follow. Any sentence that is incorrect contains no more than one error. Write both the letter and the number for all answers except (F).

(K) — faulty punctuation of restrictive
    or nonrestrictive elements
K1 — adjective clause
K2 — participial phrase
K3 — appositive
(L) — comma fault
L1 — comma alone

L2 — comma before a conjunctive adverb
L3 — comma with quotation marks
(M) — incorrect position
M1 — word
M2 — phrase
M3 — clause
M4 — appositive

F — correct sentence

1. My dog sitting on the patio barked at the robin.   ____

2. He worked until midnight, consequently, he was sleepy in class today.   ____

3. "I know you will enjoy New Orleans," he said, "The jazz sessions are fantastic."   ____

4. Doreen attends the police academy, she wants to be a state trooper.   ____

5. Aunt Kate said she will arrive at seven on the telephone.   ____

6. Henry only rode on the merry-go-round, not on the roller-coaster.   ____

7. Fitzgerald's novel, *The Great Gatsby*, has a romantic hero.   ____

8. Everyone, who is attending the Broadway play, should write for tickets soon.   ____

9. An imaginative child, hours were spent by Penny in her 'make-believe' world.   ____

10. Charlene sold an automobile that she had overhauled in her garage.   ____

N. WORDS COMMONLY CONFUSED

CORRECT WORD USAGE

Principle: There is a distinct difference in meaning between many words with similar sound and spelling.

Problem: The wrong word (basic form) is confusedly substituted for another.

INCORRECT

Eating natural foods is considered *healthy*.

> **Form Used:** *healthy* — adjective which means 'having health'

> **Form Intended:** *healthful* — adjective which means 'giving health'

CORRECT

Eating natural foods is considered *healthful*.

INCORRECT

The hikers were so exhausted that they could not walk a step *further*.

> **Form Used:** *further* — adverb indicating abstract distance

> **Form Intended:** *farther* — adverb indicating physical distance

CORRECT

The hikers were so exhausted that they could not walk a step *farther*.

INCORRECT

The company will not *except* job applications after Friday.

> **Form Used:** *except* — verb meaning 'to exclude'

> **Form Intended:** *accept* — verb meaning 'to receive'

CORRECT

The company will not *accept* job applications after Friday.

The following word-pairs are frequently confused and misused.

1. **accept, except**
accept	verb	receive
except	verb	exclude

2. **advice, advise**
advice	noun	opinion
advise	verb	recommend

3. **affect, effect**
affect	verb	influence
effect	noun	result

4. **allusion, illusion**
allusion	noun	indirect reference
illusion	noun	false image

5. **all ready, already**
all ready	adjective	completely prepared
already	adverb	before or by this time

6. **compliment, complement**
compliment	noun	expression of praise
complement	noun	something that completes

7. **council, counsel**
council	noun	assembly of persons
counsel	noun	advice

8. **continual, continuous**
continual	adjective	recurring often
continuous	adjective	unceasing

9. **disinterested, uninterested**
disinterested	adjective	impartial
uninterested	adjective	not interested

10. **farther, further**
farther	adverb	to a more distant point or space in physical distance
further	adverb	to a more distant point or space in abstract distance

11. **healthful, healthy**
healthful	adjective	giving health
healthy	adjective	having health

12. **imply, infer**

| imply | verb | suggest |
| infer | verb | conclude |

13. **loose, lose**

| loose | adjective | free |
| lose | verb | mislay |

14. **principal, principle**

| principal | noun | chief official |
| principle | noun | rule |

15. **than, then**

| than | conjunction | used in comparative statements |
| then | adverb | at that time |

16. **their, there**

| their | pronoun | possessive form of *they* |
| there | adverb | at or in that place |

17. **to, too**

| to | preposition | toward |
| too | adverb | very |

18. **were, we're**

| were | verb | past form of verb *to be* |
| we're | contraction of pronoun and verb | we are |

19. **whose, who's**

| whose | pronoun | possessive form of *who* |
| who's | contraction of pronoun and verb | who is |

20. **your, you're**

| your | pronoun | possessive form of *you* |
| you're | contraction of pronoun and verb | you are |

Proofreading for (N) Errors
Word Choice (ch)

With the aid of the chart below, identify the errors in the sentences that follow. Any incorrect sentence contains no more than one error.

N — word choice
F — correct sentence

1. The engine ran for five consecutive hours and made a continuous roar. _____

2. The team is already for the next game. _____

3. The disinterested observer left the meeting early; she was bored with the agenda. _____

4. The speaker inferred in his speech that we should exercise regularly. _____

5. The principals of the subject are known to the student. _____

6. The young child cried, "Mother, my tooth is lose." _____

7. Jack is taller then Phil. _____

8. A direct object is a sentence complement. _____

9. The city counsel met to discuss the zoning laws. _____

10. What affect will the new law have? _____

11. His mother cannot accept the fact that he is no longer a child. _____

12. Please give me your advise immediately. _____

13. In her novel she made an illusion to a Shakespearean play. _____

14. There home is near Albany, New York. _____

15. The principal is not eager to attend the conference. _____

16. Who's car have you borrowed? _____

17. Were going to study psychology in the seminar. _____

18. Your going to the game, aren't you? _____

19. She walked farther into the forest than she had intended to walk. _____

20. I know we're going to enjoy the art festival. _____

O. TAUTOLOGY (Repetition)

BREVITY

Principle: Effective writing should be clear and concise.

Problem: Unnecessarily repetitious words, phrases, and clauses obscure the clarity.

INCORRECT

In my opinion I think that we should protect agricultural land from development.

> **Repetitious Forms:** *in my opinion*
> *I think*

CORRECT

In my opinion we should protect agricultural land from development.

or

I think that we should protect agricultural land from development.

INCORRECT

Every single individual member should work to raise money for our club.

> **Repetitious Forms:** *every*
> *single*
> *individual*

CORRECT

Every member should work to raise money for our club.

COMPARISON

Principle: A comparison can be made between elements equal in function, form, and *meaning*.
Clue: *than, as*

Problem: Comparisons are made illogically between unequal elements.

or

Comparisons are stated incompletely.

INCORRECT

The teacher's short stories are more highly detailed than the student.

Illogical Comparison: *stories* — things
with
student — person

CORRECT

The teacher's short stories are more highly detailed than the student's (short stories).

or

The teacher's short stories are more highly detailed than those of the student.

INCORRECT

This new text is fully as interesting and far more instructive than any other I have thus far read.

Incomplete Comparison: *as interesting (as)*

and

more instructive than

CORRECT

This new text is fully *as interesting as* and far more instructive *than* any other I have thus far read.

INCORRECT

Phil is taller *than* any student in the class.

> **Illogical Comparison:** *Phil* — a student in the class
> with
> *any student* — in the class
> Phil cannot be taller than himself.

CORRECT

Phil is taller than any *other* student in the class.

Proofreading for (N), (O), and (P) Errors

With the aid of the chart below, identify the errors in the sentences that follow. Any incorrect sentence contains no more than one error.

N — word choice   P — faulty comparison
O — tautology   F — correct sentence

1. Statistics indicate that college board scores this year are lower than last year.   ____

2. Every single citizen should register to vote.   ____

3. Arizona is considered a healthy state.   ____

4. The town accountant has all ready issued a financial statement.   ____

5. Rhode Island is smaller than any state in the U.S.   ____

6. Continuous interruptions frequently delayed band rehearsal.   ____

7. The author's style is different from other writers.   ____

8. Edward said he would not attend the lecture because he is disinterested in geology.   ____

9. Let's look further into the issue before we reach a decision.   ____

10. This film is as interesting and far more humorous than any other I have seen.   ____

REVIEW

Proofreading for (I) — (P) Errors (#1)

With the aid of the chart below, identify the errors in the sentences that follow. Any sentence that is incorrect contains no more than one error. Write both the letter and the number for all answers except (N), (O), (P), and (F).

(I) — fragment	(L) — comma splice
I1 — dependent clause	L1 — comma alone
I2 — infinitive phrase	L2 — comma before a conjunctive adverb
I3 — participial phrase	L3 — comma with quotation marks
I4 — appositive	(M) — incorrect position
(J) — faulty reference	M1 — word
J1 — vague reference	M2 — phrase
J2 — ambiguous reference	M3 — clause
(K) — faulty punctuation of restrictive	M4 — appositive
and nonrestrictive elements	N — word choice
K1 — adjective clause	O — tautology
K2 — participial phrase	P — faulty comparison
K3 — appositive	F — correct sentence

1. Ted cannot join the ski team; he is only a beginner, a newcomer, a novice. ____

2. Freda wrote that she had visited the United States in her journal. ____

3. Only Lillian knew the answer; Dora failed to solve that problem. ____

4. Bill is an inveterate reader, he reads books, magazines, and newspapers constantly. ____

5. Because Candice reviewed her Spanish notes in a cursory manner. She failed the Spanish test. ____

6. Richard believed his new calculator would be a panacea for all his problems in mathematics, however, he soon learned differently. ____

7. Although Sara had not traveled widely, she received a vicarious pleasure from hearing her friends talk about it. ____

8. He wore a coonskin cap on his head which was too small. ____

9. "The principle rule in this game," said Kelly, "is that one must always be honest." ____

10. Dave's myopia is becoming a problem, he must purchase glasses immediately. ____

11. "Lois is a gregarious cheerleader," said the coach. "She really enjoys attending area competitions and meeting students from other high schools." ____

164

12. To manipulate a puppet skillfully. A puppeteer must be adept.　　　——

13. Armand painted a picture of two horses galloping in the art class.　　——

14. Only Elvi saw the accident; she did not see the parade.　　——

15. "Give whoever asks, the advise," said my teacher.　　——

16. Andrew opened the door quietly, however, Jeannette still heard him enter the room.　——

17. Helga was appointed to the executive board which pleased her parents.　——

18. The philatelist knew that he had received important advice; he eagerly added the new stamp to his collection.　——

19. "It is obvious," she said, "that the professional's opinion in this matter is more accurate than the layman."　——

20. The ornithologist told Chet that he should study Audubon's drawings of birds.　——

REVIEW

Proofreading for (I) — (P) Errors (#2)

With the aid of the chart below, identify the errors in the sentences that follow. Any sentence that is incorrect contains no more than one error. Write both the letter and the number for all answers except (N), (O), (P), and (F).

(I) — fragment	(L) — comma splice
I1 — dependent clause	L1 — comma alone
I2 — infinitive phrase	L2 — comma before a conjunctive adverb
I3 — participial phrase	L3 — comma with quotation marks
I4 — appositive	(M) — incorrect position
(J) — faulty reference	M1 — word
J1 — vague reference	M2 — phrase
J2 — ambiguous reference	M3 — clause
(K) — faulty punctuation of restrictive	M4 — appositive
and nonrestrictive elements	N — word choice
K1 — adjective clause	O — tautology
K2 — participial phrase	P — faulty comparison
K3 — appositive	F — correct sentence

1. She admits she is not a champion swimmer, but her sister really enjoys it. ____

2. Have you read John F. Kennedy's *Profiles in Courage*? It is a collection of short biographies. ____

3. The tourists saw many elephants stomping wildly from the tower. ____

4. Have you studied the works of Chaucer? The father of English literature. ____

5. The driver education instructor told George that he had received a special driving award. ____

6. Anna made a dress on her sewing machine which she sold to a dress shop. ____

7. My new car which is parked across the street is a Corvette. ____

8. Playing chess is great fun, you should try it some time. ____

9. Hank worked quickly, however, he failed to complete the inventory. ____

10. My St. Bernard is larger than any dog in our neighborhood. ____

11. We pondered in our minds the solution that she had offered. ____

12. "I have obviously implied," said the speaker, "that you should follow my suggestions." ____

13. We implied from the professor's lecture that his course will be extremely challenging. ____

166

14. To follow Thoreau's advice. You must simplify your life. _____

15. Because she had learned that sunflower seeds are healthy, Darlene purchased some seeds in the health food store. _____

16. While Gena was working in the automotive shop. Her brother was typing in the business department. _____

17. The work that you must study is Lorraine Hansberry's *Raisin in the Sun.* _____

18. Only Christine read Charlotte Bronte's novel, *Villette;* the other students read her novel *Jane Eyre.* _____

19. Priscilla was a disinterested observer, she didn't care which child won the music competition. _____

20. Attempting to save the disabled ship. The Coast Guard worked through the night. _____

REVIEW

Proofreading for (I) — (P) Errors (#3)

With the aid of the chart below, identify the errors in the sentences that follow. Any sentence that is incorrect contains no more than one error. Write both the letter and the number for all answers except (N), (O), (P), and (F).

(I) — fragment
I1 — dependent clause
I2 — infinitive phrase
I3 — participial phrase
I4 — appositive
(J) — faulty reference
J1 — vague reference
J2 — ambiguous reference
(K) — faulty punctuation of restrictive and nonrestrictive elements
K1 — adjective clause
K2 — participial phrase
K3 — appositive

(L) — comma splice
L1 — comma alone
L2 — comma before a conjunctive adverb
L3 — comma with quotation marks
(M) — incorrect position
M1 — word
M2 — phrase
M3 — clause
M4 — appositive
N — word choice
O — tautology
P — faulty comparison
F — correct sentence

1. The antique dealer finally sold me the Grecian vase. Although he wanted to keep it for himself. ____

2. The teacher tacked the picture on the bulletin board which I had cut from a magazine. ____

3. Maria refused to participate in the physical activities, consequently, she failed her physical education course. ____

4. We learned that the epidemic had subsided on the morning news show. ____

5. Anya is certainly as competent or more competent than her cousin Molly. ____

6. Ramone is certainly more sophisticated than Charlotte. ____

7. She only appreciated the symphony of Beethoven, not the symphony of Mozart. ____

8. Marcia explained to Gloria that she could not babysit on Sunday. ____

9. To be prepared for a hurricane. One should take the necessary precautions. ____

10. Walking along the beach and collecting sea shells. Jennie is totally happy. ____

11. If I were at the San Diego Zoo now, I would observe the peacocks, the penquins, and the pelicans. ____

12. My science teacher said that Africa is the native home of zebras. Striped animals that look like horses.   _____

13. Lions, which live only on water and meat, often prey on zebras.   _____

14. Gorillas enjoy eating bananas, a gorilla in captivity often lives for thirty years.   _____

15. "Did you realize," asked my teacher, "that the red kangaroo of Australia can run at least twenty miles per hour?"   _____

16. The jaguar is a carnivore that lives on deer and other small animals, it frequently hunts for food at night.   _____

17. The African elephant is the largest land mammal in the world; each day it eats about six hundred pounds of greenery.   _____

18. We watched the bear throwing peanuts from the zoo's touring bus.   _____

19. The largest amphibian in southern Africa is the African bullfrog. A frog that may reach a length of eight inches.   _____

20. As we delve farther into the study of animals, we become fascinated with many species.   _____

REVIEW

Proofreading for (A) — (P) Errors (#1)

With the aid of the chart below, identify the errors in the sentences that follow. Any incorrect sentence contains no more than one error.

A — lack of parallelism
B — improper case
C — lack of agreement (subject-verb)
D — lack of agreement (pronoun-antecedent)
E — dangling element
F — correct sentence
G — double negative
H — improper tense, sequence, mood
I — incomplete sentence (fragment)

J — improper pronoun reference
K — faulty punctuation of restrictive or nonrestrictive element
L — comma splice
M — incorrect position (misplaced modifier)
N — words commonly confused
O — tautology
P — faulty comparison

1. Mrs. Westfall teaches English at Hilltop High School, in her classes she always emphasizes word study. ____

2. There cannot be any doubt, I really believe, but what Mrs. Westfall teaches us vocabulary. ____

3. For example, in our English class we learned that a bibliophile is a person who loves books, however, an anglophile is one who loves England. ____

4. He studied the Stanislavsky system of acting. A method in which an actor is taught to submerge his personality into a particular role. ____

5. Entering the fashionable New York jewelry store Tiffany's, the diamonds and rubies met my gaze. ____

6. I believe, Meredith, that you are extremely competent; therefore, I will insure that every one of your work assignments are challenging. ____

7. Polly, my college roommate, is not only quick-witted but also affable. ____

8. Everybody except Beth and me was surprised to hear of Rachel entering the Peace Corps. ____

9. After a business consultation with Mr. Green, Mr. Livingston told him that he will be leaving the company in July. ____

10. Everybody but Kim and her know that the new principal will arrive on Friday. ____

11. The more one studies Latin, the more aware you become of its relationship to English. ____

12. Last evening Henry studied algebra after he finished his book report. ____

170

13. We were amazed to hear that all passengers, scheduled for Boston, were rerouted to New York. _____

14. Mr. Carter can't help believing that only his son Paul is a scholar; his other sons dislike studying. _____

15. Leona was a disinterested observer of our class discussion; she found the study of political systems boring. _____

16. Patrick, an ardent history student, is now writing a biography of the life of Julius Caesar. _____

17. There is little doubt that William is more enthusiastic than any student in the French class. _____

18. Last evening we attended a musical show and then ice-cream sodas were enjoyed by us. _____

19. The judge, a disinterested mediator, finally told the two teenagers that they can make restitution for the stolen goods. _____

20. I have a picture of a man hoeing a garden in my study. _____

REVIEW

Proofreading for (A) — (P) Errors (#2)

With the aid of the chart below, identify the errors in the sentences that follow. Any incorrect sentence contains no more than one error.

A — lack of parallelism
B — improper case
C — lack of agreement (subject-verb)
D — lack of agreement (pronoun-antecedent)
E — dangling element
F — correct sentence
G — double negative
H — improper tense, sequence, mood
I — incomplete sentence (fragment)

J — improper pronoun reference
K — faulty punctuation of restrictive or nonrestrictive element
L — comma splice
M — incorrect position (misplaced modifier)
N — words commonly confused
O — tautology
P — faulty comparison

1. This new dictionary, with its charts, graphs, illustrations, and pronunciation guides, contain 55,000 entries. ____

2. Hugh is one of those editors who have made hundreds of television appearances. ____

3. To strengthen and enrich your vocabulary, experience with words is necessary. ____

4. Annoyed with the students who failed to submit compositions on time, the English teacher assigned the following topic. Procrastination and its negative results. ____

5. After spending months in the tropics, indolence was experienced by Jan and her. ____

6. The teenage idol not only was arrogant but also boorish. ____

7. Experienced professional men are seldom effected by the opinions of callow youth. ____

8. I saw an illustration of a coyote howling in my new unabridged dictionary. ____

9. When only five years old, his parents brought him to Vienna to see the Lipizzaners, a famous breed of horses. ____

10. After the child finished the nursery project, the teacher read her the fairytale *Little Red Riding Hood*. ____

11. Pearl was surprised to learn that Venus is the Roman name for Aphrodite. The Greek goddess of love. ____

12. Every single individual member of this team should strive for excellence. ____

13. His cousin Vera is the only one of those dancers who have been a member of the Rockettes. ____

14. Everyone knew he to be the articulate spokesman of our cause. _____

15. The erudite scholar lectured on genetics, however, most of her students refused to accept her conclusions. _____

16. My dictionary, with its thousands of entries, is far more comprehensive than Aaron. _____

17. A charming raconteur, Uncle Vin told stories to his many nephews who could not help but enjoy tales of his traveling in Africa and his learning native rituals. _____

18. Everyone entered their buggies in the annual race. _____

19. Nicole's dialogues are often inane which bores everyone. _____

20. The immaculate child refused to except the chocolate ice-cream cone. _____

REVIEW

Proofreading for (A) — (P) Errors (#3)

With the aid of the chart below, identify the errors in the sentences that follow. Any incorrect sentence contains no more than one error.

A — lack of parallelism	J — improper pronoun reference
B — improper case	K — faulty punctuation of restrictive or nonrestrictive element
C — lack of agreement (subject-verb)	
D — lack of agreement (pronoun-antecedent)	L — comma splice
E — dangling element	M — incorrect position (misplaced modifier)
F — correct sentence	
G — double negative	N — words common confused
H — improper tense, sequence, mood	O — tautology
I — incomplete sentence (fragment)	P — faulty comparison

1. "He is obviously an eccentric old man," she said, "He often spends weeks absolutely alone in his summer cottage."   ____

2. Father adviced us children to be frugal, honest, and hard-working.   ____

3. The eager amateurs succeeded not only in bungling the job but also to annoy the customers.   ____

4. After they spoke to the student body, the student leaders canvassed the community for votes.   ____

5. The quixotic hero is he, the idealistic visionary who wants to change the world.   ____

6. "Don't be a martinet," she said. "Nobody wants a leader who is too strict."   ____

7. We studied the plight of the alienated hero in our literature course.   ____

8. The young actress will charm everyone because of her ebullience and because she is witty.   ____

9. Tanya borrowed a thesaurus from Adam, she wanted to study a treasury of words.   ____

10. The literary dictionary, with its definitions of such terms as *allegory, irony, parable,* and *motif,* are a necessary tool for college.   ____

11. In her business class she learned that a cartel is an international syndicate, its goal is monopoly.   ____

12. Everyone opened their government text and prepared to outline the second chapter.   ____

13. Without hardly a whisper, the little girl left the classroom and reported to the principal's office.   ____

14. Testmakers frequently try to confuse students by interchanging the following two words. *Entomology*, the study of insects, and *etymology*, the study of word origins. ____

15. The thief absconded with the company payroll which angered all of the employees. ____

16. She wanted to write her own autobiography about the story of her life. ____

17. In her lecture the speaker made an allusion to the Shakespearean play, *Macbeth.* ____

18. "We're sorry to inform you," said the salesperson, "that the manager said we cannot hold the sale on Friday." ____

19. If she were in Japan now, she would find that food prices there are higher than the United States. ____

20. On entering the department store, the unusual mannequin was observed by many shoppers. ____

BONUS ACTIVITIES (A) — (P)

1. Applying Positive Principles

—Write extra credit compositions which show that you can apply the grammatical principles effectively. Focus, if you wish, on a particular grammatical principle in each composition.

Example: *Parallelism (A)*
Write a speech that includes many examples of parallel structure. Choose a topic which arouses strong feelings.

Example: *Introductory Elements (E)*
Submit a composition that includes examples of at least three different introductory elements. Underline each element used.

—Bring to class examples from the media that illustrate effective use of positive principles. For example, find a magazine advertisement that employs effective parallelism. Note: This activity could become the basis of a class contest.

2. Finding Media Mistakes

—Bring to class some "classic" examples of errors you have observed in television commercials or in local newspapers. Note: This activity could become the basis of a class contest.

3. Gaining Proofreading Practice

—Spend a class period with a partner or as a member of a small group. Exchange papers and proofread for grammatical errors. See page 177 for a complete list of correction symbols; see page 178 for a sample composition that has already been proofread. Be sure to give positive recognition for grammatical principles employed effectively. Revise the paper before submitting it for credit.

4. Creating Exaggerated Examples

—Make a poster that illustrates a common error. Include both the incorrect sentence and the correct sentence. Note: *Common Errors (E)* and *(M)* make especially humorous examples.

PROOFREADING SYMBOLS

The following proofreading symbols correlate with the common errors:

//	lack of parallelism (A)
ca	improper case (B)
agr	lack of agreement (C-D)
dang	dangling element (E)
dn	double negative (G)
t	improper tense (H)
frag	fragment (I)
ref	improper reference (J)
p	error in punctuation (K)
	Note: p is used for any error in punctuation
cs	comma splice (L)
mp	misplaced modifier (M)
arr	arrangement (M)
ch	error in word choice (N)
w	error in word choice (N)
d	diction (N)
wdy	wordy (O)
rep	repetitious (O)
red	redundant (O)
fc	faulty comparison (P)

The following symbols are also important:

p	error in punctuation
sp	error in spelling
rs	run-on sentence
	(two or more complete thoughts run together without punctuation marks)
cap	error in use of capital letters
k	awkward
¶	paragraph
no ¶	no paragraph
u	lack of unity and logical thinking
var	variety
emp	emphasis
nc	not clear
ms	error in manuscript form or neatness
∧	omission of words
coh	lack of coherence

SAMPLE COMPOSITION

The speaker: a student
The audience: the speaker's classmates
The topic: writing a composition

The Secret of Successful Composition

Have you ever sat in an English class and shuddered at your English teacher's announcement: "Now, class, the next composition will be due on Friday"? Have you, at that point, imagined yourself once again sitting wearily at your desk, chewing on a number-two pencil, and to stare at a piece of blank composition paper? If you have ever experienced this, relax now and take the advise of a former worrier, who has found the secret of successful composition. Surprisingly, this secret consists of two simple actions: finding the right subject and to follow a specific approach.

Although their are many "places" to find a composition topic — libraries, books, the media. There is one absolutely foolproof place to find your right topic. That place is located within you. Do you realize that your mind is an inner file containing your personal and individual ideas and feelings. Do you realize that your everyday thoughts contain hundreds of composition topics related to your experiences at home, at school, and working? Study, for example, the following three questions:

1. What is the most beneficial course in your school?
2. How can your hobby become your livelihood?
3. What do you think is the greatest advantage that your (school, job, hobby, or extracurricular activity) has to offer you?

Your answer to any one of these questions are the basis of a unique composition.

You must agree that finding the right topic is easy. You simply look within yourself for an individual interest. You then ask yourself an important question about this interest, finally, you make the answer to this question the main idea, the thesis, of your composition. If you choose your hobby as your interest, for example, you might ask yourself the following question: How can I make my hobby my livelihood? You might answer as follows: I can make my hobby, reading, my livelihood, by operating a bookstore which contains hundreds of books to read on the job and to discuss with interested customers.

You following a specific approach is even easier than the right topic. You simply ask yourself a few more questions like the following: What do I know specifically about my subject that no one else knows? What concrete, colorful details can I use to interest my reader? If reading is your hobby, for example, what titles and topics will support the idea that reading on the job is enjoyable?

178

What kind of "interested" customer will discuss books enthusiastically? Your specific answers to such questions will lead you to the right approach.

You now have the secret of successful composition. You now realize that *rep* writing a composition can be an interesting, adventurous exploration of your mind. The exciting discovery of yourself. Who knows? You may even respond to *frag* your English teacher's next composition announcement as follows: "Will I *sp* recieve extra credit for submitting two or three compositions?"

APPENDIX A

Review Chart of Sentence Functions
(Parts of Speech)

Verb (Predicate)	States action	$\overset{s}{Tom}$ $\overset{v}{threw}$ the ball.
	States being	$\overset{s}{Tom}$ $\overset{v}{is}$ a pitcher.
	Note: See *Appendix B* for additional information on the verb.	
Noun	Names a person	The $\overset{n}{girl}$ is intelligent.
	place	Plan to visit $\overset{n}{Washington}$.
	thing	He drove the $\overset{n}{car}$ recklessly.
	quality	$\overset{n}{Courage}$ is a virtue.
	idea	$\overset{n}{That\ she\ will}$ win is obvious.
	action	He likes $\overset{n}{skiing}$ and $\overset{n}{swimming}$.
Pronoun	Stands for a noun and therefore names.	$\overset{pro}{She}$ is present.
	There are many types of pronouns.	$\overset{pro}{I}$ know $\overset{pro}{who}$ $\overset{pro}{he}$ is.
Adjective	Modifies a noun or a pronoun.	The $\overset{adj}{successful}$ student enjoys life.
		He is $\overset{adj}{successful}$.

Adverb	Modifies a verb, an adjective, or an adverb.	The woman walked *slowly*. (v → adv) She was *extremely* tired. (adv → adj) He talked *very* loudly. (adv → adv)
Preposition	Joins its object to some other word(s) in the sentence.	She walked *to* the concert. (p / obj)
	A word is a preposition only if it has an object.	He fell *down* the stairs. (p / obj) He fell *down*. (adv)
	The preposition and its object form a word group called a prepositional phrase.	He fell *down* the stairs. (adv; p / obj)
Conjunction	Joins words, phrases, and clauses.	The students study + *and* play.
	Coordinate conjunctions (and, but, or, nor, for) join words, phrases and clauses of equal value.	She worked in the library + *and* at home. + He studied French, *and* then he played tennis.
	Subordinating conjunctions join elements of unequal value.	*When* she entered the room, she saw the painting. (sc)
Interjection	Exclaims	*Wow!* It's great.

APPENDIX B

Additional Information on the Verb

Verb (Predicate)   States action

$\overset{s}{\quad}$ $\overset{v}{\quad}$
Tom *threw* the ball.

States being

$\overset{s}{\quad}$ $\overset{v}{\quad}$
Tom *is* a pitcher.

Verb Phrase
A verb phrase consists of two or more words used as the verb of the sentence. It is formed by combining a principal part of a verb of action or being with one or more helping verbs.

Example: Tom *is throwing* the ball. (v phrase)
Helping Verb: *is*
Principal Verb: *throwing* — present participle of *to throw*

Principal Parts of Verbs
All verbs have four forms which are called principal parts.

Principal Parts	*Action Verb*	*Being Verb*
1. present infinitive	walk	be
2. present participle	walking	being
3. past tense	walked	was
4. past participle	walked	been

Common Helping Verbs
The main helping verbs are as follows: is, am, are, was, were, be, being, been, has, have, had, do, does, did, shall, will, should, would, may, must, might, can, could.

Tense Formation
The various verb tenses can often be formed by the combination of a principal part of a verb and a helping verb. See the Chart on page 116. See Page 63 for a distinction between a *regular verb* and an *irregular verb*.

NOTES

Introduction
1. Percy Marks, *Better Themes* (New York, 1933), p. 73.

Part I Sentence Awareness
1. Percy Marks, *Better Themes* (New York, 1933), p. 73.
2. Herbert Read, *English Prose Style* (Boston, 1955), p. 33.
3. Otto Jespersen, *Language* (New York, 1964), p. 438.
4. Jean Piaget, *The Language and Thought of the Child* (New York, 1973), p. 146.
5. Theone Hughes and Jean Malmstrom (eds.) *Who's Afraid of Linguistics?* (Michigan, 1968), p. 23.
6. _____, *Proper Words in Proper Places*

Part II Sentence Analysis
1. John Hodges and Mary E. Whitten, *Harbrace College Handbook* (New York, 1967), p. 10.
2. Ibid., p. 3.

BIBLIOGRAPHY

To make a definite statement of bibliographical sources for this system would be impossible, for it represents a synthesis of materials compiled during almost twenty years of teaching. I am obviously in debt to the *Harbrace College Handbooks* by John Hodges, various editions of *English Grammar and Composition* by John Warriner, and Earl Wood's *Junior* and *Senior English Review Exercises*.

Hodges, John C. *Harbrace College Handbook*. 4th ed. New York: Harcourt, Brace and Company, 1956.

Hodges, John C. and Mary E. Whitten. *Harbrace College Handbook*. 6th ed. New York: Harcourt, Brace and World, Inc., 1967.

Hughes, Theone and Jean Malmstrom (eds.) *Who's Afraid of Linguistics?* Michigan: Michigan Council of Teachers of English, 1968.

Jespersen, Otto. *Language*. New York: W. W. Norton and Co., Inc., 1964.

Marks, Percy. *Better Themes*. New York: Harcourt, Brace and Company, 1933.

Piaget, Jean. *The Language and Thought of the Child*. New York: World Publishing, 1973.

_____ . *Proper Words in Proper Places*.

Read, Herbert. *English Prose Style*. Boston: Beacon Press, 1959.

Warriner, John E. and Francis Griffith. *English Grammar and Composition*. Revised ed. New York: Harcourt, Brace and World, Inc., 1965.

Wood, Earl. *Junior English Review Exercises* and *Senior English Review Exercises*. Cambridge, Massachusetts: Educators Publishing Service, 1977.

ADDITIONAL SOURCES CONSULTED

The following books were consulted as general references during the writing of this book.

Bernstein, Theodore M. *Miss Thistlebottom's Hobgoblins*. New York: Farrar, Straus and Giroux, 1971.

Christensen, Francis. *Notes Toward a New Rhetoric*. New York: Harper and Row Publishers, 1967.

Hupp, Alice. *The Mechanics of the Sentence*. New York: American Book Co., 1937.

Nurnberg, Maxwell. *Questions You Always Wanted to Ask About English*. New York: Washington Square Press, 1972.

Opdycke, John B. *Harper's English Grammar.* New York: Popular Library, 1965.

O'Rourke, L. J. *Self-Aids in English Usage.* Florida: The Psychological Institute, 1951.

Pooley, Robert C. *The Teaching of English Usage.* Urbana, Illinois: National Council of Teachers of English, 1975.

Shostak, Jerome. *How to Prepare for College Board Achievement Tests: English.* New York: Barron's Educational Service, Inc., 1974.

Strunk, William and E. B. White. *The Elements of Style.* New York: The MacMillan Co., 1972.